About the Book

"Dr. Stevens brings us a fresh and illuminating approach to self-mastery. She uncovers specific laws of nature that govern our lives and gives us step-by-step guidelines for discovering how to live in harmony with them."

— Jack Canfield, co-author, *Chicken Soup for the Soul*

"*Unlimited Futures* is a compilation of Dr. Stevens' lifelong experience developing the philosophy and techniques that she teaches in the courses which she and her husband, Dr. Dean Portinga, have given to thousands of fortunate people. Incorporating diverse elements of psychology and philosophy, she has created a pragmatic approach that is now presented in very understandable terms for everyone. As I read this thorough text, I re-experienced the course that I took with them some years ago. I would encourage anyone who wants their life to be more fulfilling to read this book over and over."

— Steven Hollenbeck, M.D., family physician

"No human goal is more important than that of realizing the potential for self-actualization and achieving it. *Unlimited Futures* gives you all of the tools you need to reach your goals."

— C. Norman Shealy, M.D., Ph.D., founder, *Shealy Wellness Center,* founding president, *American Holistic Medical Association*, and author of twenty-six books and numerous scientific papers

"Through research and discovery, Bobbie Stevens has developed a seven-step process for creating an ideal life. This process has changed my life! *Unlimited Futures* gives step-by-step instructions and examples so you, too, can enjoy an ideal life. The information in this book is priceless!"

— Joan E. Gustafson, president, *Success and Leadership Dynamics,* author, *A Woman Can Do That! —10 Strategies for Creating Success in Your Life*

"Our beliefs, accumulated over a lifetime, often get in the way of our possibilities. Bobbie and the *Unlimited Futures* course has helped me, my wife, my employees and many others to release the power that we all have within us to give our gifts to the world, to our loved ones, and to ourselves."

— John Christensen, CEO, *ChartHouse Learning,* co-author, *Fish*

"Bobbie Stevens has managed to map out a road to higher consciousness that not only inspires us as to where we can go, but most importantly, how we can get there. Her specific practices for turning these grand ideas into directed action will empower and energize anyone who is serious about experiencing the frontiers of personal potential."

— William G. VanArsdale, executive producer, *Inner Voyages* TV series

"*Unlimited Futures* is a complete and compelling source for anyone who is interested in developing a higher, more fulfilling and purposeful life. Dr. Bobbie Stevens writes in an easy-to-read style, including many examples and practical exercises. This book reflects her insight and talent in teaching others how to manifest goals and desires in keeping with spiritual principles. I highly recommend *Unlimited Futures* as a valuable guide."

— Jack Kern, minister

"Discover your true purpose in life and how to fulfill it. Become a self-actualized human being with *Unlimited Futures*. This book is a powerful and practical guide to personal transformation. Read it and leap!"

— Chef Jerry Bartholow, author,
Peace Soup—The Recipe for a Peaceful Life in the New Millennium

"With *Unlimited Futures*, Bobbie Stevens creates a design for creating a higher spiritual awareness."

— James Redfield, author, *Celestine Prophecy*

What course participants say about the *Unlimited Futures Course*

"The *Unlimited Futures* course is life-changing. No longer do you react to life, you take charge of creating your ideal life with powerful new insights and tools to do so! There is an immense awakening regarding who you are, how you function and why you are here. Everything in your experience is wonderfully transformed, enhanced and changed on every level through this new expanded awareness. This knowledge and these skills absolutely bring my life greater peace, joy and meaning as it continues to unfold perfectly according to my vision. I am so very, very grateful for this exquisite experience."

— Cheryl O'Shaughnessy, business owner

"I have had two severe heart attacks—the last one was two months before I was introduced to the *Unlimited Futures* course. Without this course I would probably not be alive today. I have gained more and more, better and better health, ever since I began my first program with *Unlimited Futures* fifteen years ago. My focus was on my health and it has improved beyond my ability to imagine before this course. I now focus on whatever I want, and I easily see golden opportunities."

— Robert M. Cargill, retired grain executive

"The course is a complete process for creating anything I desire in my life. I have learned to really expand my vision of what is possible and how to move through any obstacles I think exist."

— Mary Jo Walter, accountant

"I have found that the principles and practices from the *Unlimited Futures* program allow me to deal with normally stressful situations in a calm and effective manner. I believe anyone would find it to be a growth experience that would adapt to their specific needs."

— Ken Larson, CEO, *Polaris Industries, Inc.*

"My participation in the *Unlimited Futures* core course has helped me to make some very important changes in my life externally, and more importantly to me, internally. The simple fact that I actually know what my ambitions and desires are automatically brings some stability and contentment to my life. But watching those desires become fulfilled is an inspiring experience, and I have just scratched the surface."

— Michael Johnson, recording artist

"The opportunity to join this 'creative process course' came at a time of unprecedented stress in my life. It provided me support equal to the stress by means of new knowledge, practical methods and a framework for what I knew already and what I will come to know. In the end I learned how to create the life I want. As a physician, trained in the sciences, the connection to quantum physics was most helpful. With the five basic choices I now move through life with much greater awareness and intentionality than before. I am a helper who is now more adept at giving help and receiving help."

—Milton H. Seifert Jr., M.D., family physician

"I learned that the energizers are so important in order to open up the energy flow. I learned to relax more and let things happen without getting stressed. I love this course. I have taken it four times and could keep taking it because every time I get something different."

— Jean Ketcham, business owner

"The *Unlimited Futures* course is extraordinary. It has brought me to a new level of goal achievement, enjoyment of life, focus on purpose, and abundance in all ways. Through living the seven steps in the creative process I am well on my way to creating a life of choice rather than chance."

—Tara Tuck, educator

"Profoundly powerful and hard to describe. The best thing I have experienced in forty-five years. Puts consulting in a very different realm."

— Patrick Powers, Ph.D., business consultant

"Areas of my life that I felt were good before and really didn't need improvement, have become great. Personal relationships are stronger and more open than ever before. Prior to the course, I viewed my job as low stress—however, it would take forty-five to fifty hours a week to accomplish what needed to be done. During the course I discovered my body was holding a large amount of stress, and my beliefs about my job were not correct. After completing the course . . . I have minimized my time at work and increased my productivity."

— Glenn Myers, vice president, *Giefer Sales Company*

"Once the stress was released by doing the exercises in the course, many, many exciting events happened. Life turned joyful, my vision of the future became very clear. Learning that what is going to happen will come totally from inside me is a wonderful life learning experience."

— Michael Ketcham, business owner

"The greatest gift in life is to remain in fully recognized and realized connection to your source. In this course and the continued practice of this program you can, in fact, establish this and become an unfolding picture of all your dreams."

— Ronald W. Jensen, psychologist/minister

"WOW! What a life changer the *Unlimited Futures* course has been for me. It has brought a better and working understanding of the many self-help books I have read. I understood the ideas, but taking the *Unlimited Futures* course has enabled me to implement the ideas in a practical way with tangible results. It is difficult for me to imagine anyone taking this course seriously and not coming away a changed person. Thank you for making such an enriching experience available. In gratitude,"

—Landon Kite, Jr., CEO, *Quantum Management Associates, Inc.*

A Word about the *Unlimited Futures Executive Development Program*

"In my personal view, these are some of the most important attributes of good leaders:

- good judgment and decisiveness
- creativity and intuitive insight
- vision for the enterprise
- ethics and responsible choices
- motivation of self and others
- effective interpersonal relationships
- creation of team spirit and high morale

Leadership traits are, in turn, dependent upon more fundamental capabilities:

- improving stress management
- quieting the mind
- increasing focus and concentration
- accessing intuitive awareness
- uncovering and replacing self-limiting beliefs
- discovering our personal vision and mission

These underlying capabilities are strengthened through the *Unlimited Futures Executive Development Program*, so that leadership traits become second nature. The corporation gains a much more effective leader, while the individual becomes more successful and finds greater enjoyment in success."

—Alan Norton, director, *3M Corporation*

UNLIMITED FUTURES

HOW TO Understand the Life you Have & Create the Life you Want

Bobbie Stevens, PhD

SELF-PUBLISHED BY
THEUFB.COM

ISBN: 978-1-60585-086-3
Cover, typesetting and book design: DLD, Inc.

Published by
THEUFB.COM

Dedication

to Dean Portinga,
my best friend, husband
and business partner,
along with
ALL Unlimited Futures
course participants.

Contents

Foreword

Bobbie Stevens gives us a comprehensive view of how life works, combining age-old wisdom with current knowledge in becoming a self-actualized person. *Unlimited Futures* lays out a clear path to transformation with practical methods and techniques for creating the lives we want in a better world. The book teaches the principles of a higher order and inspires us to commit to our soul's purpose. With personal anecdotes and information from great minds, Dr. Stevens explains how to eliminate self-defeating habits in expanding our physical, mental, and spiritual creative potential. *Unlimited Futures* is a book to keep close at hand, to read, study, remind, and practice its steps for manifesting the self you were meant to be.

— Jane Kern, Ph.D., Educational Leadership Consultant and author, *Inventing a School: Expanding the Boundaries of Learning*

Acknowledgments

In this second edition of my book—I have many people to thank for the success of the first printing. First, I want to thank all of the people who have participated in the *Unlimited Futures* courses over the years. Thank you for sharing your lives with us, and giving me the opportunity to test and prove over and over again the value of this program. Thanks, too, for helping to spread the word of the great possibilities that are available to all of us.

I want to express my sincere appreciation to Dean and Timm Lockhart, who have brought our endeavors to share this knowledge to a whole new level. Dean, through his communication and design talents, has impacted all our work. He is responsible for the enhanced book design, its cover and our new image. My deepest gratitude goes to Timm for his internet marketing expertise and taking the lead to see that many more people will be able to receive the blessing of owning this book. He is responsible for this second edition and getting it out into the world.

My thanks and appreciation also goes to Paul Scheele and Pete Bissonette for introducing my work to their clients at *Learning Strategies*. Paul and Pete experienced our core course just as they were starting their business many years ago, and have been loyal supporters ever since. I am grateful for their continued support.

I would also like to acknowledge a great group of people who participated in a very special *Personal Growth and Development* course and have provided so much support ever since. They are: Kevin and Michelle Sheridan, Cheryl O'Shaughnessey, Patricia Varley and Ed Zimmerman.

A special thanks goes to Sid Williams, who, after attending one of our courses, decided to use his video skills to tape a core course which we plan to make available on the internet in the future. My appreciation goes to the participants of the course who are: Dr. Patricia Primero, Orlando Tamayo, Bridget Egan, Darlene Davies, Diane DeCaro, Chalmers Brothers, Michael and Gina Weiley, and George Walmsley. Others that I want to acknowledge for their contributions in helping our work move forward are: Jayme Check, Michael Grubb, Barry Curtis, Kathleen Boyle, Mike and Jean Ketcham, and Joan Gustafson.

Last, but not least, I want to express my appreciation to my husband, Dean Portinga, who always supports me fully in whatever I choose to do.

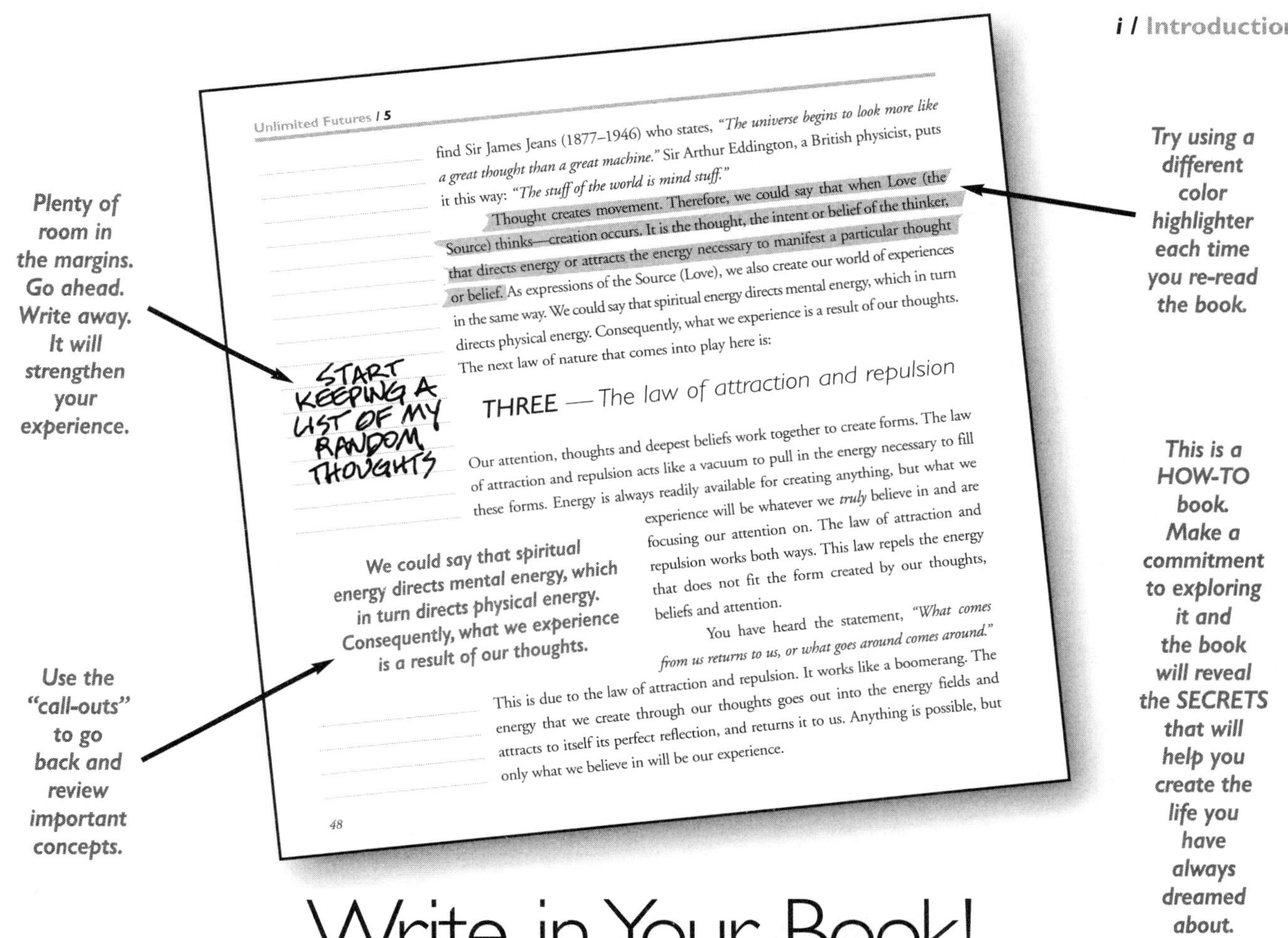

Unlimited Futures / 5

find Sir James Jeans (1877–1946) who states, *"The universe begins to look more like a great thought than a great machine."* Sir Arthur Eddington, a British physicist, puts it this way: *"The stuff of the world is mind stuff."*

Thought creates movement. Therefore, we could say that when Love (the Source) thinks—creation occurs. It is the thought, the intent or belief of the thinker, that directs energy or attracts the energy necessary to manifest a particular thought or belief. As expressions of the Source (Love), we also create our world of experiences in the same way. We could say that spiritual energy directs mental energy, which in turn directs physical energy. Consequently, what we experience is a result of our thoughts. The next law of nature that comes into play here is:

THREE — The law of attraction and repulsion

Our attention, thoughts and deepest beliefs work together to create forms. The law of attraction and repulsion acts like a vacuum to pull in the energy necessary to fill these forms. Energy is always readily available for creating anything, but what we experience will be whatever we *truly* believe in and are focusing our attention on. The law of attraction and repulsion works both ways. This law repels the energy that does not fit the form created by our thoughts, beliefs and attention.

We could say that spiritual energy directs mental energy, which in turn directs physical energy. Consequently, what we experience is a result of our thoughts.

You have heard the statement, *"What comes from us returns to us, or what goes around comes around."* This is due to the law of attraction and repulsion. It works like a boomerang. The energy that we create through our thoughts goes out into the energy fields and attracts to itself its perfect reflection, and returns it to us. Anything is possible, but only what we believe in will be our experience.

48

Write in Your Book!

Some of the information in this book will be new to you. Some, you may have heard before. Our intent is that you *own* it all for yourself—that this becomes *your* information.

1. Make notes. Writing enhances memory and cognitive functioning.
2. Read the book more than one time. After you start working the program and your nervous system begins to release stress, you will experience the book *differently* each subsequent time you read it.
3. Go to the website: ***www.ufb.com*** to get tips and tools to help you more effectively interact with the information in this book.

Introduction

The ills from which we are suffering have had their seat in the very foundation of human thought. But today something is happening to the whole structure of human consciousness. A fresh kind of life is starting. There is for us in the future not only survival, but superlife.

—Teilhardde Chardin, The Phenomenon of Man

Unlimited Futures is about the *"superlife."* What would the superlife be like? Have you ever wondered how it would be if you were totally in charge and could create every aspect of your life just the way you would like it to be? What would you create?

Most of us would want to be perfectly healthy, full of energy and vitality. Our minds would be clear and sharp. We might even be brilliant or, at least, highly intelligent. We would probably look good and have a pleasant personality. The people in our lives would respect and love us. All of our relationships would be happy and harmonious, and we would create a loving, intimate relationship with someone special. We would create a career that provided interesting, fulfilling work, which would allow us to use our many talents. Then, we would be sure we had all the money we needed to buy the material things we wanted in our lives, like a beautiful place to live, great clothes and luxury transportation. This would be a good start, right?

Even though most of us could agree on some of these things—if we were able to create them in our own lives, they would look very different to each of us. That is because they *mean* something very different to each of us. By now you are probably saying, *"What's the point? Let's get real. I have the life I have and I don't know how to change it. Things just happen. I don't know why. I just do the best I can."*

Many years ago when I first started college, I began to wonder why some people are so much more successful than others in all areas of life. What is the key to happiness, fulfillment, wealth? People I asked told me things such as—*"It's hard work," "high IQ," "connections," "luck."*

As I looked more carefully at these assumptions, they proved incorrect. I knew some people who worked hard and gained a certain degree of success, but there were others who worked hard and showed little or no success. I knew people with high IQs who were doing well, and others with high IQs who led very disappointing lives. The same proved to be true with connections. Since none of us know exactly what luck is, it is hard to rule it out, however, it doesn't seem to offer much help in understanding the question.

I knew there had to be an answer. It seemed to me that there was a huge gap in human knowledge, and I was determined to find out what was responsible for the choices we make and the resulting experiences.

Since my major was psychology, I eventually found the works of Abraham Maslow. He was the first psychologist to study psychologically healthy people. Before Maslow's studies, the entire field of psychology was focused on observing psychologically sick people.

Maslow noticed that there were some people who functioned on a totally different level than most other people he knew. He decided to study these people to discover what made them different. These *very* healthy people saw the world from a totally different perspective. They were highly intuitive. They had the ability to know things from a source that others were not able to access. They saw beauty and order, and experienced life from a different dimension than other people. Maslow said they lived peaceful, joyous lives and made significant contributions to the world. He coined the term *"self-actualized"* to describe the way these people functioned.

Maslow reported that these self-actualized people had transcended needs. They had discovered the ability within themselves to fulfill their *own* needs and desires. Maybe Maslow's observations could be the answer to my question. If some people lived from this more advanced level, then it must be a potential for all of us—a *human potential.* Maslow observed that the people who lived on this advanced plane were different, and studying them gave him some great insights into the higher level of functioning that they demonstrated.

My next question was *"How does one become self-actualized?"* It seems that some people are simply born with these abilities. However, I knew that they must be innate abilities that could be developed. My hope was to discover how it all worked. For many years I looked for answers, but didn't find a clue.

In 1968, I finally discovered the answer to my question. It seemed to be quite by accident, but now I know it was no accident at all. I began an experiment to find a way to quit smoking, but discovered much, much more—a process for developing self-actualization.

In the first part of this book, I share with you my experiment and how it worked for me. After many years of experimenting with the process and proving its validity over and over again, I designed a program to help others develop their potential. I then founded *Unlimited Futures,* a company that provides this program. Thousands of people have attended these *Unlimited Futures* courses over the years, with outstanding results. I will share some of their experiences with you. We came to understand one simple truth—that self-actualization is an automatic result of high-level health or wellness.

In *Part Two,* we explore what self-actualization is. We look at the characteristics that Maslow found in the self-actualized people he studied. We also discover why we are not all self-actualized. We look at some basic laws of nature that govern our lives. They are laws that are affecting us all the time. Once we understand how they work in our lives, we can then see how and why we experience the things we do—how we create our own experiences. We explore how choice works, and who gets to make the choices. We learn how to create optimal health and live in harmony with the laws of nature that govern our lives.

In *Part Three,* we lay out a process that will bring us to higher levels of health, wellness and self-actualization. It is a process that takes place over time. So many are looking for a quick fix, but to my knowledge, there isn't one. The beauty of this process—this new lifestyle—is that one's health and life continues to get better and better. We discover that we really *can* take charge and create the kind of life we have always longed for.

In *Part Four,* we compare how the ordinary person perceives and handles life's situations with how the self-actualized person responds. We look at our personal lives, relationship situations, and the differences in how the ordinary person and the self-actualized person each function in the workplace. In the last chapter of *Part Four,* we project how society will change as more people become self-actualized.

Just reading this book will *not* change your life. It is important to *choose* to make the *commitment* necessary to follow the program guidelines and experience the results for yourself. No one else can do it for us. It doesn't matter how many books we read, how many tapes we listen to, or how many courses we attend—it is all *just information* until we choose to implement it into our own lives.

We all have certain things that we do regularly as a result of our beliefs. This combination of habits and actions form what we call our *lifestyle.* We become quite comfortable in our lifestyles, believing that this is what we need to continue doing to create the life we want. However, as we look at the laws that govern our life experiences, we may realize that we need to make some changes. When it comes to change, we just start from wherever we are. By following the guidelines in *Part Three,* and making an active commitment, we can watch a transformation take place in our lives.

An example of a transformation is seen in the process of a caterpillar becoming a butterfly. The worlds of a caterpillar and a butterfly are very different realities. The caterpillar is *worm-like* as it inches its way along trying to feed itself and survive in a very small world, usually just a few yards of space.

The butterfly, on the other hand, can fly. Its world is very large. Butterflies can fly thousands of miles and some even travel internationally. The butterfly's world is one of freedom and ease. They do not need to struggle to find food, feeding from the sweet nectar of flowers just for the taking. And they provide a valuable service, by effortlessly carrying pollen from flower to flower. They fulfill their purpose of bringing beauty to the world—simply by *being* who they are.

Every caterpillar has the potential to become a butterfly. A butterfly is just a mature caterpillar. The caterpillar, in its immaturity or undiscovered potential, struggles along trying to fulfill its needs by doing the best it can. However, in the process, it can damage crops and is considered a nuisance. Once they reach their full potential, by becoming butterflies, they are able to fulfill all their needs without harming anything. They live a life of freedom, ease and abundance as they realize their purpose, and make their contribution to the world.

This much-expanded reality is the result of a transformation process that is necessary for the caterpillar to reach its potential and become a butterfly.

This is a parallel analogy to what we as people experience in discovering who we are, and actualizing our potential. This book is about understanding how you can go through your own transformation process.

The process itself, just as with the caterpillar, is an internal one. People do not look as drastically different outwardly as do butterflies from caterpillars. For us, this is an inner process that takes place in our thoughts, beliefs, actions and experiences, it is certainly no less spectacular than that of the caterpillar. We, too, create a much-expanded reality for ourselves. We discover a whole new world. Within each of us lies the potential to expand our horizons, fulfill our needs, create the life we want for ourselves, fulfill our purpose and make a wonderful contribution to the world. Just like butterflies, we can live lives of freedom, ease and abundance.

This book is about you—who you are, how you function, your purpose and how to accomplish it.

My purpose in writing this book is to share this knowledge of possibility and transformation. I provide step-by-step guidelines anyone can use to create a lifestyle that will bring greater health, happiness, love and fulfillment into your life. I write this with the deepest gratitude for the revelation to me of this knowledge, and the wonderful opportunity to share it with you. May you be as abundantly blessed as I have been.

And as a final note, I would like to challenge someone to come up with a new pronoun that means either male or female. I tried to use "they," but *"they"* told me that it was not grammatically correct when speaking of just one person. This left me with no alternative but to follow what writers have done in the past—to use the pronoun *"he"* to mean both male and female. We need a new word. In fact, we need a number of new words. If you find your purpose is to help clarify our language, please accept this challenge!

PART ONE 1

Breaking the Limits

One

1

My Search for the Meaning of Life and Discovery of a Whole New World

No barriers, masses of matter however enormous, can withstand the powers of the mind—the remotest corners yield to them—all things succumb; the very Heaven itself is laid open.

—Marcus Manilius, Roman author, c. 40 B.C.

The year was 1968 and I was living alone for the second time in my life. My first experience was not a good one. I was very lonely and not at all prepared for having that much time to myself. This time I was determined to make it work. It was the perfect time to take stock of my life.

I am an only child, but always had many friends to keep me company. My parents owned several small businesses, which I worked in as I was growing up. I got married right out of high school, and started my work career. My better judgment told me to go to college, but all of my friends were getting married. It just seemed to be the thing to do.

I got married mostly to keep from hurting my boyfriend, which seems ridiculous now, but at the time I didn't know what else to do. We had very little in common, and the marriage ended in divorce four years later. I felt sad, of course, but mostly I felt a great sense of freedom. Now, I could choose who I wanted to be, the career I wanted to pursue, and a whole new life for myself. Then came the question: "What do I want to do with my life?" There were so many things to think about—so many possible choices I could make.

I had often wondered why some people are so successful while others fail. Somehow I knew that it was more than having a good education, a high IQ or just being lucky…

I was very much interested in business, and was, at the time, going to business school at night. After getting my degree in accounting, I seriously considered taking the exam to become a CPA, but soon realized that I was much more interested in working with people than numbers.

I had often wondered why some people are so successful while others fail. I heard all the different theories floating around. Some people believed it was education—if you get a good education you will be successful. Others said you needed a high IQ. Neither theory seemed plausible to me. I knew people who were highly educated yet were not what I would consider successful. Others belonged to MENSA, but couldn't even get a job. There had to be something else, and I wanted to know why some people are so much more successful than others in all areas. It also seemed to me that most problems in life were related to the way we think. This discovery sent me back to school to study psychology.

College was fun for me even though I worked full time. The study of psychology, however, was not what I had hoped it would be. Our curriculum was mostly in the field of abnormal psychology, but my interest was in the *field of possibilities*. I wanted to know what was different about people who lead happy, successful lives and made significant contributions to the world. After a few years of pursuing psychology, it became obvious that I would not be learning the answers to my questions there. It was time to rethink the direction of my life. There had to be something more rewarding to do than study abnormal psychology.

Modeling school sounded like a good idea. I decided to try it, and it was indeed fun. Our teacher had us listen to and work with a recording by Earl Nightingale, which gave us instructions for creating whatever we wanted. We were to set our goals, write them down and look at them every day. Then we were to act upon whatever came to us to fulfill our goals. She said we should experiment with this technique, and that we really could accomplish our goals, whatever they were.

Our teacher believed there were only two career choices that made sense for women at the time, either modeling or becoming an airline stewardess (as it was called in those days). Traveling appealed to me, and so did the idea of meeting lots of interesting people. Since I was too short to be taken very seriously as a fashion model outside the petite arena, I decided to become a stewardess. I followed Nightingale's instructions and accomplished all of my goals, including landing a job as a stewardess with a major airline. I felt pretty good about this since I was told they hired only one out of every hundred interviewed at that time. I vowed to continue using this procedure, but soon forgot it in all the activities of moving and starting my new career. It was all very rewarding. I met many interesting people and enjoyed visiting places I had never seen before.

We worked about eighty hours a month which gave me time to take some classes and stay involved in the business world.

There was so much I wanted to understand...what is luck...where does it come from...what role do we play in creating our own experiences... how does life REALLY work?

By 1968, I had been with the airlines for eight years and had traveled around the world. It was time to take a serious look at my life. In the past, I usually had two or three jobs or major projects going at the same time. I also had an active social life, but there was something missing. I decided to take some time to be alone and ask some important questions—questions such as: "What is life really all about?", "Why am I here?" and "What should I be doing with my life?" It seemed to me that there had to be more to life than what I, and everyone I knew, understood. The meaning and purpose of life had to be more than mere survival and consumption of goods and services.

A feeling of loneliness and emptiness inside continued to persist. Most of us think that loneliness can be eliminated by having someone special in our lives, but I knew this wasn't the answer. I had been in several very special relationships, even though I was not in one at the time. I knew that if I stayed busy enough with my friendships and my work, I wouldn't have time to think about the really important questions. This was not a time for another relationship—it was a time for my *own* personal growth.

There was so much I didn't understand—things that I truly wanted to know, like why things go so well at times and then fall apart at others. What is luck? Where does it come from and why? What role do we each play in creating our experiences, and how does it work? As I was thinking on these things one day, I saw an article in a magazine about some breathing exercises that were supposed to help people quit smoking. I had started smoking after becoming a flight attendant. At that time cigarettes were served on every tray, and smoking was the "in" thing to do. All of my roommates smoked, and I joined them, but I always hated the fact that I had become addicted.

I had quit smoking many times, and once even made it for eight months. Then a crisis arose and I started again. Even when I had been able to give up smoking for almost a year, I still wanted a cigarette every time I saw someone else smoking. When I would start smoking again I would always smoke more than before. It was definitely compulsive behavior. It was as if I had to make up for the time I had lost when not smoking, as if I had a goal to smoke a certain number of cigarettes. I never became involved with drugs, but from listening to others' experiences, it seems very much the same. Now was the time to rid myself of this addiction.

I found a teacher to help me with the breathing exercises that I had read about. She also taught me some stretching exercises. Within the next few weeks, while looking for a book on stretching exercises, I found a book on focusing techniques and meditation. I put together a routine of all these things and started doing it daily. I decided to quit smoking again a few days after I started my breathing lessons. This time it was different; I had no desire to smoke again. Within a few weeks I began to feel more energetic and my mind seemed to become sharper. I thought it was just the result of freeing my body of the tar and nicotine I had been feeding it each day, and I am sure that was a major factor in the beginning.

However, within a few months I began to experience a continued increase in energy. I felt younger and more confident. In fact, my energy level was more like that of a sixteen-year-old than that of a thirty-three-year-old person. Along with this increase of energy came a very calm and peaceful feeling. I felt quite whole and complete. This was something that I had never known before. The loneliness I had felt in the past had completely disappeared. In fact, I loved being alone. I was growing by leaps and bounds. I practiced my routine of breathing exercises, stretching exercises, meditation and focusing techniques daily. I felt so great, I even decided to set aside one day a month for being completely alone. I wouldn't even answer the phone. It was a day of silence for me, where I would practice my routine, experiment and read.

As time went on, I started having very strong feelings of love. I had been in love with someone close to me several times and, of course, I loved my family. But this was different. I was in love with life. Everything seemed lighter, and I felt an inner joy. I was truly happy, and this happiness didn't relate to anyone or anything outside myself. I was not unhappy before, but this was a totally new experience for me. Somehow I wanted to express this love, and since it wasn't related to anyone in particular, it seemed to express itself through greater kindness and thoughtfulness for everyone I met. There were times when the love seemed so strong that in my mind I would simply bless people whom I had never seen before. Somehow I knew that we are all connected, and if I thought of blessing them that they would indeed be blessed.

I put together a routine of breathing and stretching exercises, focusing techniques and mediation. Using it, I was finally able to quit smoking almost immediately. Within a few weeks of practicing the routine I began to feel more energetic and my mind seemed sharper. And after a year of committing to my program, I started noticing something quite amazing.

This was a very different experience from the fast-paced, results-oriented, bottom-line, get-to-the-point-and-move-on kind of person that I had always been. Life was taking on a whole new meaning for me.

I had probably been practicing my routine each day for about a year when I started noticing something totally new—I would know something was going to happen before it actually occurred. Many times the phone would ring and I would know who was calling before I answered it. At first this was simply fascinating, then I realized that if I could know these things automatically, maybe I could use this ability to get answers to my questions. I began experimenting with this possibility—and it worked well.

My experiment started with questions that I could research and find the answers to, or at least ones that I knew *had* answers. After finishing my routine, while I was still in a very quiet place, I would ask a question. Then I would listen for the answer to come into my consciousness. Sometimes an answer would come right away, other times it didn't, but I knew it would eventually. Usually within days, sometimes weeks, the answer would *arrive.* They came in numerous ways. Sometimes the answer simply appeared in my mind, or sometimes I would pick up a book and find it there. Other times it would show up on TV, or someone would tell me the answer I was seeking. It was a most interesting experiment to notice how I always received answers, even though they came in various ways. I would always check to see if the answer was valid and always found them to be true.

I began to intuitively KNOW the answers to questions without having to struggle or search for the information.

I had many, many questions about life and how it worked. I truly wanted to understand how experiences are created, why things happen as they do, and who or what is responsible. These were questions that, to my knowledge, did not have answers, or at least not answers that I could accept as true. After experimenting with questions that I could actually verify, I decided it was time to ask these more important questions. This experiment started with the question, "What role do we each play in creating our own experiences?" At the very moment I asked the question the answer started to unfold, or appear in my consciousness. This unfoldment continued on for several months. It simply came to me and I knew that I knew—there was no doubt in my mind.

I could see that everything in existence is made of energy, and that energy is moved and directed and formed by intelligence, and that intelligence is based in love.

The love that I was experiencing was not about something external, this love was who we ALL are. I could see that Love is the power source of the universe. Love contains all intelligence and is the source of all energy. On a conscious level I was experiencing what Einstein referred to as the *unified field.* I could see that everything in the universe originates from the same source. This source, which we access through silence or stillness, described by physicists as absolute zero, is all there is.

In this place of stillness I could see that everything in the Universe is energy and that this energy is directed and formed by intelligence, and that this intelligence is based in Love.

When Love—the source—moves, energy is created. This energy is moved in an intelligent way to create all of existence. Consequently, everyone and everything is this Love, Intelligence and Energy. We are all this Oneness. Our separateness is only in form. I could clearly see that we live in a perfect universe, and there are non-changing laws of nature, or principles of life, that are responsible for how it works. I began to perceive these principles and understand how they governed the working of our lives. It was quite clear to see that given this understanding, I could create anything I wanted.

One of these principles is that ***mental energy directs physical energy.*** This concept explains how we create the experiences in our lives. We create our own experiences through our own thoughts, or more accurately, through our beliefs. Once I knew this, I could clearly see how my friends and I had created our experiences. It was really very funny, because it is so simple once we understand it. On the other hand, it was also quite sad to see the struggle and hardship that we draw to ourselves simply because we do not understand the laws of nature, or principles of life, that we are *automatically* using every day. It is like trying to play a game without knowing the rules.

We create experiences in our lives by directing physical energy through mental energy. Our thoughts and beliefs are the guiding forces that determine how physical energy forms itself.

It was clear to see that our ***beliefs are simply information that we have accepted as truth.*** Many of our beliefs have simply been programmed into our consciousness from our environment. Some have been handed down from generation to generation and many more are beliefs that have been accepted by our society as truth, and we have never even questioned them. It is a vicious circle—we have a belief about something that creates an experience, which in turn validates the belief. This is how we keep creating the same kind of experiences for ourselves over and over again. The tricky part about beliefs is that about eighty-five percent of what we believe is not on the conscious level. We don't know what we believe until we take the time to explore ourselves and bring these thoughts into our consciousness.

Beliefs are simply information that we have accepted as truth and we can change these beliefs to create what we want rather than what we don't want.

The knowledge that ***beliefs are simply information that we have accepted as truth***, and that we can change them to create what we want rather than what we don't want, was a great relief. I realized that I believed many things that were not helping me to create the life I wanted. This started the next phase of my growth. I could now see that ***the choices we make create our experiences*** and those choices are governed by our beliefs. There are truly infinite possibilities, but they are guided by the information that we accept as truth. My next project was to become aware of the many beliefs I had that were not useful to me, and to change them. This concept was not new, but, until now, I had no idea about how to actually change a belief. After practicing my program and concentrating my attention on changing my beliefs for about a month, I was now ready to start working with creating. After all, it was most exciting to know that I could create anything I wanted. The next question,

My next project was to become aware of the many beliefs I had "collected" that were no longer useful and to CHANGE them.

of course, was what would I want to create? I gave this serious thought. Where should I start? I could see that there was a process for creating anything. First I needed to decide what I wanted to create, then I needed to visualize it as being a part of my life. This visualization creates a form for the energy to move into. The third step was acceptance. This is where our beliefs come in. If I could not believe in my desire and fully accept it, the energy for its fulfillment would be repelled. Fortunately for me at that time, I was totally prepared. I could see how the process worked, and was strong and clear enough to work with it. The fourth step was to focus my attention on it. Then I needed to listen for guidance. I knew that I would intuitively know what I needed to do. I simply needed to follow through with the action and my creation would materialize. It was now time to start my first creation after understanding how the process works.

Discovering what we want and actually CHOOSING it are vital parts of the process.

What did I want? I wanted to create something on a very material level so I could easily see how the process functioned and that it did indeed work. I wanted to experience how these principles would demonstrate themselves in a business situation. I decided to create my own place to live. I was single and living alone in an apartment. I didn't want the upkeep of a house—what I wanted was a townhouse. One of the immediate problems was that there weren't any townhouses in my area. Townhouses were new at the time. I had seen them in other parts of the country, but there weren't any in Minnesota. I knew this didn't matter, it would just make the process more interesting. Once I knew what I wanted to create, I needed to clearly visualize it in my mind in as much detail as possible. I visited townhouses in other cities and got a clear image in my mind of what mine would look like. Not only did I see the number of rooms, their location and sizes, but I also bought furniture in my mind, including a grand piano, and decorated the townhouse exactly the way I wanted it to be.

I wanted this vision to be as big as I could imagine, something that I was not capable of accomplishing if I had to do things the way I had in the past. In addition to the new townhouse for myself, I decided I should also create a second townhouse to rent out for additional income. Then, I decided I should have a new car to go in my new garage, which, of course, I visualized in detail. This was as much as I could imagine at the time. The next step was acceptance. Could I accept all of this in my life now? I had already changed my beliefs to correspond with the new understanding that I now had—that ***beliefs are only information that we have accepted as truth.*** I knew, without a shadow of a doubt, that my vision would manifest and that it would all happen within a year.

My next step was to keep my attention focused on the vision until it actually manifested in the material world. I became quiet and still, and asked what I should do to help this vision manifest. It came to me that I should get a real estate license. I followed through on this guidance, studied the books, took the test and got a license. What next? The idea came that I should get a job selling real estate. Well, I didn't see how this would help, since there weren't any townhouses built in our area. I followed my guidance anyway and began reading the want ads in the paper by real estate companies looking for agents. One caught my attention—it invited people to take a test to see if they would be successful in real estate. I applied, took a three-hour-long battery of tests, and was promptly hired.

Then the challenge was to keep my attention focused on my vision until it actually manifested in the material world.

Three weeks later, my boss called me into his office and told me my test results had arrived. I asked if it showed that I would be successful in real estate. He said, yes, that I would most likely be successful, but there was something he was very concerned about in one of my answers. I immediately knew what he was talking about. One of the questions asked about how much money you expected to make your first year in real estate. Well, I had already figured out how much money I would need to buy both townhouses, furnish the one I planned to live in the way I wanted, and buy my new car, so I entered that dollar amount as the answer to the question. I knew it would raise some eyebrows, but I decided to put it down anyway. He looked at me for a few moments then asked, "Do you know how many houses you would have to sell to make that much money?" I said, "No." It was a good thing that I hadn't figured that out, or I might have doubted myself, which would have repelled the energy necessary to fulfill my vision. He told me that it took him five years of very hard work to make that much money. I finally convinced him that I wasn't crazy, but told him that this was my vision and I would keep working toward it.

To make a long story short, I earned exactly the amount I had written on the form my first year in real estate. However, I was with that company only about three months when one of the agents told me about an apartment complex that was being converted into townhouses to be sold individually. I went over to take a look, and met the developer who was doing the conversion. I asked him if he had ever thought about building new townhouses. He said he had, and was in the process of putting together his plans for a new development at that time. He told me about it, but it didn't sound like what I had in mind. I had clearly seen in my mind's eye the location, size and surroundings of the townhouse development I wanted to be in. I shared my vision with him and asked if he would consider looking for the land and building what I had envisioned. He said he was always open to new possibilities. Immediately, I knew things were coming together. I told him that I would sell the units at this location if he would build the development I had described. He was impressed with my confidence that I could sell his units. We decided to work together and my vision began to show tangible results.

I purchased one of the units in the development, decorated it, and moved in. I used it for a model until we could get one of the other units ready. It was clear to me that this would be my rental townhouse. A few weeks later the developer called me and said he had talked with a man who owned a piece of land used as a nursery, which was located in a residential area. He thought it sounded very much like what I had described to him. We looked at it, and it was exactly what I had seen in my mind's eye. The size was perfect and it had beautiful mature trees lining the entire property. It was located about ten minutes from the airport on a very beautiful residential street. This was it—my vision was manifesting.

He bought an option to buy the land. The next step was to create the plans. Sales were going very well on the conversion project, and he had started the development he was planning when we met. We needed a certain amount of pre-sales to put the financing together. This new development would have to be sold without the benefit of models. We drew up plans and created a miniature model of the complex to display under glass. That was all I needed. By this time my energy was so high and my mind was so clear that things seemed to happen almost automatically. I continued to work with the principles of creation and was delighted to see how well they worked in a business setting. Every evening I would take some time to get very clear in my mind what I wanted to happen the next day. I would visualize it, accept it, and it happened. I found people calling me or walking into my office whom I had visualized seeing or talking with the day before. My work became easier and easier. I *expected* that everyone I met would want to help me, and they did. People would buy a townhouse, then they would bring their friends to buy another one. Someone even rang my doorbell out-of-the-blue one evening and proclaimed, *"I would like to buy one of the townhouses you are selling."*

It was a small development, only twenty-seven units plus a pool and clubhouse. I sold all of them in a very short time. The developer was amazed at how successful I had been and wanted to know if I could teach others to sell the way I did.

It was obviously a different way of selling. It was quite clear to me to see why my sales were so easy and why others found it difficult. Just as with all of our experiences, we get what we expect. I knew that my vision was indeed coming about and would manifest within the year. My focus was on helping others fulfill their visions. I wanted everyone to be as happy with their townhouses as I was with mine. I would help them modify the design to fit their needs. I also assisted them with finding financing and showed them how to handle their money to make the most of what they had. I knew I was taken care of, consequently, I was not concerned with myself. I was only there to help them. This mind-set sent out an energy that attracted people to me. In observing some of the other sales people, I could see that they, too, were putting out energy. Many times it was the energy of *needing* to make a sale. The prospective customer felt the energy of someone trying to get something from them, so they protected themselves by leaving.

Just as with all of our experiences, we get what we expect.

This is how we create the problems in our lives. If we feel a need, we put out an energy that demands the fulfillment of that belief. We can never create what we want when we feel needy. In order to create the life we want for ourselves, we must feel whole and complete within ourselves. Our creations are not external—they come from within us. In my original discovery I began to feel whole and complete. I knew that I was not separate from anyone or anything else. Separateness is only in form. ***Everything in existence is love expressing intelligently through energy.*** This is a basic non-changing law of nature, or principle of life, that we must understand in order to create the lives we desire.

We can never create what we want when we feel NEEDY. In order to create the life we dream about, we must feel whole and complete within ourselves.

Two

Creating My Ideal Partner

Let all seen enjoyments lead to the unseen fountain from whence they flow.

—T.C. Haliburton, nineteenth century Canadian historian

My experiment was a success! I had worked with the principles that I had discovered and created the vision just as I had envisioned it. It had been one year since beginning this adventure and I was now living in the new townhouse—with beautiful furniture including a grand piano—decorated just the way I wanted it. I was also driving a new bronze Cutlass Supreme Oldsmobile, and the second townhouse was rented as planned. I had experienced being on top of the world. My energy had been very high, my mind very clear, and my plans and desires had materialized with the greatest of ease.

The developer I was working with had started two more projects and I was now the new sales manager. I was excited to see if I could teach others to function the way I had been functioning. However, I was experiencing a little less energy and a little less clarity, so it was becoming more difficult to keep up my usual pace. Gradually, I was moving back toward the level of functioning I had always experienced before my discovery.

I now had two full-time jobs. As a flight attendant, I could fly a trip to Hawaii, which left on Saturday morning and returned Sunday morning. I didn't work the return trip, so I was able to sleep on the flight. On Sundays my flight arrived about 7:00 A.M. I would come home from my trip, take a shower and hold an open house on Sunday afternoon. I was having so much success and so much fun that I had stopped doing the daily routine which had brought me to this new level. I knew it was time to let go of some of my activity and get back to my daily practice of the breathing exercises, stretching exercises, meditation and focusing techniques.

Circumstances seemed to take care of the situation. I had pre-sold more than enough townhouses and condominiums to secure financing for our latest project, but money had become very tight. In fact, none was available for real estate in our area due to a state law that wouldn't allow interest rates to go to the level that existed in other parts of the country. My real estate career was over for now. This turn of events gave me time to evaluate my life *again*. I found myself returning to the same questions. What is my purpose in being here and what should I be doing with my life? This time the answer came very clearly—*I should fully understand these principles and share them with others.* Sounded good, but I didn't have the foggiest idea how to even get started. When I asked about it, the answer that came was, *"When the time is right, you will know"*. For now, all I knew was that it was time to go back to my process and discover what had happened, why it happened, and how I could help others work with these principles to create what they wanted in their lives.

I finally realized what had happened to me. This routine that I was practicing on a daily basis had actually strengthened my nervous system so it was capable of a higher level of functioning.

It took several years, but I finally realized what had happened for me. The routine of things I had put together, and was practicing on a daily basis, had strengthened my nervous system so it was capable of a higher level of functioning. It was clear to me that this is our natural state, but a state I had never experienced before, nor did I know anyone else who had. What I had created through my routine was a process for releasing stress stored in the nervous system, and strengthening the system so it was capable of a more refined level of functioning. It was simply high-level wellness. I had previously believed that if I wasn't sick, and if I felt OK, I was healthy. Now, it was clear to me that there are much higher levels of health possible. And if it was possible for me, it had to also be possible for others.

I knew I had discovered something of great value. I already knew *THAT* the process works now I needed to understand *HOW* it works in order to discover a way to share it with others. I embarked on a campaign to read lots of books to gain a greater understanding of stress, the nervous system and how they interact. Everyone experiences stress in their lives. Dr. Hans Selye, who devoted his life to the study of stress, said there are two kinds of stress—he called them eustress and distress. Eustress could be called good stress, the stress necessary to keep us functioning. Distress is created when the system has become overloaded.

Dr. Selye defines stress as any demand made on the nervous system. The nervous system carries all the messages from the senses to the brain and then dispatches electrical signals to all parts of the body. Using his definition, we can see how much stress we have in our lives. There are many types of stress. Emotional stress is what we usually think of when we think of stress, but there are other kinds just as damaging. Environmental stresses come from the poor quality of our air, water and food we eat. Mental stress comes from the demands for our attention constantly coming from all directions at the same time. And stress based in safety and security is rampant in a world so filled with fear. When the nervous system becomes overloaded, it simply stores the demands until it has time to catch up. This is similar to the way an office worker would stack paperwork on his desk when he had more than he could handle. Over time, we can see how this would create problems.

An overloaded nervous system, caused by too much "stored up" stress, creates an imbalance where the mind is no longer communicating effectively with the body.

This stored stress prevents the mind-body system from functioning at its full capacity. The accumulation takes place over time and is such a gradual process that we never notice it. Most of us begin overstressing the nervous system while we are still children, therefore, we never know the full capacity of the nervous system as an adult. If the system was not over-stressed, a good night's sleep would take care of revitalizing it, so it could function at its peak capacity. Since most of us have grossly over-stressed the system all of our lives, it takes additional repair

Given sufficient amounts of rest, the body releases stress and strengthens itself. But the levels of stress that we carry in our modern day lives is far more than the mind-body system can release in a simple night's sleep.

to bring it back to its natural state. As doctors will tell you, our bodies know how to heal and strengthen themselves if given the time to do so. When we are sick, the first thing a doctor will tell us is to get plenty of rest. Given a sufficient amount of rest, the body releases stress and restores itself. There is so much stress in our lives that unless we make a conscious effort to reduce it, stress continues to mount. Gradually, we have less and less energy at our disposal and our minds aren't quite as clear as we need them to be. But we never notice, because this is also happening to others, and we think it is natural, or at least inevitable—if we think about it at all.

The process of doing the breathing and stretching exercises, along with meditation and the use of the focusing techniques, released the stress that had been stored in my nervous system. It also strengthened the system so that it was capable of functioning much more effectively. This more refined functioning of the nervous system automatically connected my conscious awareness with intuitive knowingness. I came to understand that ***intuition is a natural capacity of a strong nervous system.***

Nothing in my background had prepared me for this—it just happened. I started wondering if others also had such experiences. Again, I went back to psychology and discovered Abraham Maslow's work. Up through the 1950s, the field of psychology had been dominated by the study of psychologically *sick* people. Maslow was the first to study psychologically *healthy* people. Through his research he discovered a few people who functioned differently than most of the population. He called these people ***self-actualized.*** *They lived their lives from a much higher level of health than most.* Maslow found that they were highly intuitive and creative. In reading more of Maslow's studies, I realized he was describing the same kinds of experiences I had been enjoying. I was not alone, and knew I had discovered something valuable—a process for helping others release

Intuition is a natural capacity of a strong and healthy nervous system.

stress, strengthen the nervous system and actually move into a new world from what most of us experience. I knew I must find a way to share this.

My friends knew something wonderful had happened for me and they wanted to understand it. They were asking how they could also experience this. I didn't know. I tried to explain it with words, but it didn't help much. I had to create a course that would give them an experience of their own. I told them things to try, but without a full understanding of the process they were not able to follow through on their own. I knew that when the time was right I would know how to share this knowledge, but that didn't keep it from being quite frustrating while I waited and searched for an answer on how to open it up to others.

Self-actualized people function from a much higher level of health and awareness than most people.

What I had intuitively known from the beginning was that I must experiment with this process in my own life until I fully understood how it worked. It was probably time to use the creative process again for myself. "What do I want?" I was single and truly wanted someone to share my life with. Everything had changed so dramatically, and I longed for someone to share all aspects of it with me. I knew my life would be about these new discoveries and I wanted to explore it with someone who was as excited as I was with my discoveries. I didn't know anyone who had any knowledge of this kind of thing. However, I did know that I could attract someone into my life who would be perfectly suited to me in every way. I simply needed to get clear on what that person would be like. I knew he existed, but I needed to first know him in my mind in order to attract him into my life.

If he were perfectly suited for a relationship with me where we could share our work and life together, what would he be like? First, he would have some knowledge about the kind of things I am now working with, plus a very strong interest in this field. He should probably be a psychologist. It would also be good if he had some background in business. He would be intelligent and good looking *(of course)* and also be fun to be with. I can get pretty focused on work, so he should like fun things to help me stay light. He would also be curious—an explorer. He would enjoy handling some details, such as planning vacations. He would be very supportive and easy to live with. He would be thoughtful and considerate. We would love each other deeply, and he would appreciate me for being who I am. It would be a very special relationship and everyone we met would be inspired by it.

I worked with my vision until I got as clear as I could about my future partner. I tried to cover all the bases because I knew if I didn't get clear, whatever beliefs I held on a deep level, would indeed show up. Once I was as clear as possible, I created visions of the two of us being together, working, exploring and having fun.

Next, I had to check my deep beliefs. My girl friends and I held similar ideas. We would say things like, *"There just aren't any good men around"* or, *"Why can't I meet someone really special?"* This, of course, assumed that anyone I would want to be with didn't exist or at least wasn't going to be in *my* life. Time to reprogram that kind of thinking. I knew that these negative ideas didn't need to be true. They were simply something that we had accepted and were creating in our lives. Even though I had been consciously exploring my beliefs for years, they still needed some work. I continued to review them until I felt I could fully accept this ideal person in my life and fully expected him to appear at any minute.

I knew that when I didn't get as clear as possible about what I wanted, it was more likely that limiting beliefs deep within my subconscious could interfere with what I was creating.

It took a little time, but guess what? He showed up. I was at a spiritual retreat for a weekend, and when I came down the stairs to the dining room for dinner, I noticed a very good-looking man observing me. Most of the people at the retreat were younger than I, but he was obviously older and looked most interesting.

It was a buffet serving, and when I got in line I noticed him right behind me. We started talking in line and then sat together for dinner. He told me that he was a psychologist, but was now in the business world. He had grown up in a family business, just as I had. After a few years in business with his father and brother he decided to go back to school, where he received doctorates in both theology and psychology. When his father retired he and his brother inherited the family business. The business, however, no longer motivated him, and he was at a crossroads in his life. I told him a little about myself and he seemed interested. We walked to class and sat together. When the class was over I went back to my room, but I couldn't stop thinking about him. I thought of all the reasons why he probably wasn't the one. He was ten years older than I, and I had never dated anyone that much older before. The age difference was too much, and there were probably other reasons, but I still wanted to get to know him better anyway. I finally went to sleep, but woke up a couple of times with the same thought—is he the one? I couldn't wait to get to class the next day. He was there, saving a seat for me. He asked me out for dinner on the Sunday night after the course was over. I invited him to follow me back to my townhouse after classes on Sunday afternoon. I needed to return calls from some real estate ads I had placed in the paper before going out to dinner. He thoroughly investigated my townhouse while I made my calls. Yes, he was definitely an explorer.

We have now been married for twenty-eight years, and have spent very little time apart since that snowy Sunday in Minnesota in 1977. I shared with him my discovery and he was most interested. I found that he had a lot of knowledge about these things, but his understanding was strictly on an intellectual level, even though he had seen what appeared to be miracles take place in his work. He knew that knowing something on the intellectual level is quite different from actually experiencing it in one's own life.

I knew the process I had gone through required a dedicated focus over time.

He would be the perfect experiment, and he wanted to try it. I taught him the breathing exercises, stretching exercises and focusing techniques. He had already started to meditate on a regular basis. We practiced our routine together and he began to have some of the same experiences. This was a time of change for him. Dean was phasing out of the family business and didn't know what he wanted to do. I told him he could create whatever he wanted, and he was ready to try. He had a huge résumé and was serving on the board of directors for several companies. He had started to put out some feelers about possibilities, and was trying to go in a dozen different directions at the same time. I explained the need for one-pointed focus, the creative process, and that we need not concern ourselves with what appeared to be available. I knew anything was possible. What he needed to do was get clear on what he wanted.

After going through a lot of soul searching, reading *What Color Is Your Parachute?* and doing some exercises for getting clear, he finally said to me, *"What I would really like is to have enough money at my disposal to research how the physical, mental and spiritual aspects of life interrelate."* Along with that description he also informed me that this kind of opportunity didn't exist. I assured him that it would, *once we created it.* Dean continued to work on the vision, getting clear about where his office would be, the surroundings, how much he would be paid, etc. I helped him work with his vision, challenging his beliefs, until we had both accepted it and expected it to happen. And sure enough, it did.

A couple of months later he was scheduled to speak at a conference in Houston, Texas, to a large audience of business executives from around the country. His subject was creativity in business. I joined him for the trip and we talked about the real possibilities for business innovation. By now we both fully understood that everyone is connected to the source of all intelligence, and that it was possible to tap into this intelligence and know intuitively whatever we wanted to know whenever we chose. We were not at all sure the business world was ready for this, but he decided that he would tell them anyway.

We had a great trip, and the audience was very receptive. A few days after we had returned to Minneapolis, he got a phone call from the director of research and development for a large company based in Tacoma, Washington. He said that he and others from their company had been in the audience in Texas and had been introduced to many new terms they had never heard before. They wanted to know more about *"creative intelligence."* They asked if Dean could meet them at the airport in Minneapolis to discuss it further. He agreed, and asked me to join them. We met in the Top Flight Club for about two and a half hours. They left us with an invitation to visit with them at their headquarters in a couple of weeks.

The company had beautiful offices and we were very much impressed with their research and development department. They were well aware of the changes that were taking place in the world today, and were preparing for the paradigm shift. They already knew about the benefit of meditation and had plans for meditation rooms for their employees. We discussed intuition and how it could work in the business world. They asked Dean if he knew any CEOs who were using intuition to make their business decisions. He replied that he did. They concluded that this was a spiritual phenomenon, and thought that they should assemble what they were calling a spiritual advisory board, made up of highly intuitive people, to advise them.

I offered my understanding that intuition is not a way of gathering abstract information. My experience was that what comes to us intuitively is related to what we truly want to know. I was not able to intuitively know anything that was not related to what I personally needed to know. I explained that we are all naturally intuitive and can develop these abilities. My suggestion was to develop the individual intuitive abilities of the people involved in the business. The meeting concluded with their request that we decide what needed to be done.

Dean was ready to start putting together a board of highly intuitive people. I knew that wouldn't work. It would be far more effective to develop a program to help people connect to their own intuitive abilities. We were discussing what to do on the flight home, when Dean picked up a copy of *Corporate Report* magazine that happened to be in the seat pocket. The cover story was about Lynn Charlson, a Minneapolis businessman who had used his intuitive abilities to invent products and create a very successful company. He was considered to be the father of fluid hydraulics. Dean was determined to meet Charlson and called shortly after we returned home. He was well protected from the public, however, and it took about a month of calling until one day Charlson answered the phone himself. Dean explained that he had been very impressed with the article in *Corporate Report* and would like to meet with him. They set a time.

Lynn Charlson, was the founder and president of the Char-Lynn company. He and Dean had a great time at their meeting, discussing each other's backgrounds and common interests. Charlson told him that he grew up on a farm in North Dakota, came to Minneapolis while still in his teens and worked as a night clerk at a local hotel. It seems that a number of engineers stayed at the hotel and he listened to them talking about their problems and needs. He came to realize that he could intuitively sense how to solve their problems, and to the amazement of the engineers, his suggestions worked. After he became proficient with this skill, he raised enough money to start his own engineering company. Although he hired some well-educated engineers to work for him, Charlson would go out to the farms and talk to the farmers about their needs himself. Then he would come back to the office to meditate on the problem. A three-dimensional solution would then appear to him in his mind's eye. He would take it to his engineers and they would undoubtedly say it couldn't be built. However, he knew it could, because he had already seen it in his mind. Many times he would have to put together a prototype himself because his engineers couldn't believe it until they could see it. This was how all his patents had come about.

Dean was very much intrigued, and loved talking with him. They were both curious about how this process worked. A couple of weeks later he called Dean over to his office for a visit. He had sold his company, and now wanted to create a research foundation which would explore how the physical sciences, mental sciences and the spiritual aspect of life relate to each other. He asked Dean if he would like to be the director of the foundation.

This was it—exactly what Dean had been focusing his attention on creating. Lynn Charlson had become very wealthy from all of his patents, and his foundation was designed to do exactly what Dean wanted to do. They agreed to work together and the details unfolded perfectly.

Dean worked with the foundation for seven years, and they spent millions of dollars doing some very fine research and working with a number of universities and other organizations. Even though this was valuable work, Charlson's desire was never fulfilled. He wanted to teach others how to tap into their own intuitive abilities as he did. By combining this ability with their intellectual education, these students could become far more creative, bringing greater innovation to business and the world. The foundation conducted many workshops over the years, but even though participants learned new concepts, nothing seemed to change in their lives.

Charlson was very fortunate to have had such a natural capability, but he didn't know how to develop it in others. I, on the other hand, had *not* been born with this intuitive ability, but had discovered a way to develop it within myself, and had now been able to share it with someone else—Dean.

3 Three

Creating a Process for Sharing

Man's capacities have never been measured, nor are we to judge what he can do by any precedents, so little has been tried.

—Henry David Thoreau

I was serving on the board of directors for an organization that I really hoped would succeed. The president was having problems communicating with the board. There were a number of different views about the purpose of the organization and the direction it was to take. They were also in conflict as to who should be the leader. I knew that if everyone could see the situation more clearly, things could be worked out to the satisfaction of all, or we could at least devise a plan that would work for the greatest good of the organization.

For many years I had known that I must put together a program for sharing my discovery, and now was the perfect opportunity to design one and test it. I believed I could set up a course to teach the board members the same process I had used to reach a level of much greater clarity. And we could then save the organization.

It took a couple of months to design the course. By the time it was completed several board members had resigned, but the remaining ones agreed to participate. I knew it was a process that would take place over time, but didn't know how much time was needed. It was about total commitment and choosing to devote the time necessary to learn and integrate the routine into their lives to create a whole new way of living. There had to be a definite commitment and enough time to create new habits.

The Charlson Research Foundation was investigating the significance of numbers. The number seven seemed to mean fullness and completion. I didn't know how many sessions the course would take, but seven seemed like a good enough number for me. It also seemed that we should have seven participants for this pilot study. Since there weren't seven members left on the board, I decided to invite a few friends to join us in the experiment. I told the participants that I knew it would be possible for all of us to increase our energy, think more clearly, and create anything we wanted. They were all excited to try the program. I told them it would require at least an hour every day to do the stretching exercises, breathing exercises, meditation, focusing techniques and working with our choices. They all made a commitment to show up every other week for a three-and-one-half hour class over seven sessions and do the assignments every day.

Since schedules had to be changed several times, our three-and-a-half month experiment lasted almost six months! The time frame was less important to me—I was far more interested in results. And the successes generated by all the participants exceeded even *my* wildest expectations. First, each participant became very clear about what they wanted to create in their lives. The question they each asked themselves was the same one that I had asked Dean, "If you knew you could create anything you wanted, what would it be?" We worked through a variety of techniques to help them get as clear as possible. I asked them to each come up with seven things they wanted to create in their lives within the next three months. I told them to forget about figuring out *how* they were going to create it—just get clear about what they *would* want if there was *nothing that could stop them* from creating it.

It was fun watching them break free from fears and old beliefs, and even more fun watching them create their dreams and desires.

It was fun watching them break free from fears and old beliefs, and even more fun watching them create their dreams and desires. The class was made up of a variety of personalities, occupations and desires. There was a stockbroker, a bank vice president, a manufacturer's representative, a flight attendant, an administrative assistant, a salesman and a real estate broker.

By the end of the course each person was experiencing life on a different level. They had all manifested the seven things they wanted to create, or at least were able to see that they had made great strides in moving toward them. They were so excited about their experiences that they wanted to share them with family and friends, and asked me to do another class. That was in 1984, and that was the beginning of *Unlimited Futures*. Since that time, thousands of people have participated in the course with wonderful results.

In the meantime, Dean and I were creating our dream house. I knew my purpose in life was to share my discovery with others, and now I had created a program that would allow me to do just that. We knew we would need a place to hold the courses, so, with the understanding of the importance of environment, we created a home with offices, classrooms, a pool, a tennis court, and walking paths within a forest of beautiful trees on a lake. It was *spectacular*—a place we wanted to share with others—exactly what we had envisioned. Now, we were all set. For years, Dean and I knew that we wanted to work together in business, so in the summer of 1985 he left the Research Foundation and came to work with me at *Unlimited Futures*.

By the end of the course, each participant was experiencing life on an entirely different level.

The company grew. Through taking the course, more and more people were discovering their own ability to take charge of their world and create the life they wanted for themselves. I also designed the *Executive Development Program* so we could share the course with people in many of the major corporations within the Twin Cities.

This is NOT a three-month course. It is a LIFETIME experience. It is about understanding basic laws of nature, principles of life, and living in harmony with them to create the life you've always desired.

We realized that we had something of great value and wanted the opportunity to share it with more and more people. The question was *how*. Again, I learned that life, for each of us, is about our own personal growth. Just as in the beginning when I first started working with these techniques, I found it took much longer than I had hoped to discover how to share them with others. I knew there needed to be a way for a person to take the course over and over until it had become totally integrated into one's life. This is not a three-month course, it is a lifetime experience. It was about understanding some basic laws of nature, or principles of life, and living in harmony with them—about taking charge of our lives and creating them the way we want them to be. It is a lifetime process for all of us. Each achievement brings us to the next challenge, but it is most gratifying to know that we can meet this new challenge, and that soon it will become another accomplishment.

This discovery has been the most natural and fulfilling experience of my life. It has not been just one experience, but an ongoing one that has allowed me to take charge of my life and create the life that I continuously choose for myself.

We now know that each of us has the potential to create whatever we choose. Whether we want to create inner peace and joy for ourselves, happy fulfilling relationships, a successful career that is rich and rewarding, wealth, or the perfect mate—the principles work the same way in each case. We simply have to know these principles and prepare ourselves to be capable of working with them to create whatever we want.

It is all about taking charge of our lives and creating them the way that we want them to be.

PART TWO 2

A New Paradigm / A New World

Four

What is Self-Actualization?

The goal of education...is ultimately the self-actualization of a person, the becoming fully human, the development of the fullest height that the human species can stand up to...

—Abraham Maslow,
twentieth century American psychologist

Abraham Maslow speaks of a self-actualized person as one who is psychologically healthy or mature. Here is a list of some of the characteristics that Maslow found in the self-actualized people he studied.

1. They are healthy—physically, mentally, emotionally and spiritually.
2. They are superior in their perception of reality, which results in an advanced ability to reason and perceive truth. The consequence is that they live more in the *real world of nature* rather than in the *man-made world* of mass media, abstract concepts, pre-formed expectations, and the accepted beliefs and stereotypes that most people confuse with the *real world.*
3. They are more accepting of self, others and nature. They find it possible to *embrace* themselves and their own nature without chagrin or complaint or, for that matter, without even thinking about the matter very much. They see human nature as it is and not as they would prefer it to be.
4. They exhibit spontaneity, simplicity and naturalness. Because of this, they have codes of ethics that are relatively autonomous and individual rather than conventional.
5. They are solution-centered rather than ego-centered. They customarily have some mission in life, some task to fulfill, some quest outside themselves, which enlists much of their energies.
6. They have a quality of detachment and a need for privacy. They can be solitary without harm to themselves and without discomfort. Most enjoy this solitude to a greater degree than the average person. It is possible for them to remain above the battle—unruffled and undisturbed by issues that produce

turmoil in others. They find it easy to be aloof, reserved, calm and serene—thus it becomes possible for them to take personal misfortunes without reacting as the ordinary person does.

7. They are quite autonomous, independent of culture and environment. They are in charge of their own lives, active agents of their own will.
8. Self-actualized people have an on-going freshness of appreciation. They have the wonderful capability to appreciate, again and again, the basic *goodness* of life. They look at the world with awe, pleasure, wonder and even ecstasy, however stale and mundane it seems to others.
9. They are highly intuitive and many of them have had *"peak experiences"* which have allowed them to see the entire universe in its fullness as an integrated and unified whole.
10. They are compassionate.
11. In interpersonal relations, they are capable of more *fusion,* greater love, more perfect identification, more obliteration of the ego boundaries than other people would consider possible.
12. They are democratic characters. They are friendly with anyone of suitable character regardless of class, education, political belief, race or color. It often seems as if they are not even aware of these differences.
13. They have unusual powers of discrimination. These individuals are strongly ethical—they have *definite* moral standards. They do right and do not do wrong. Needless to say, their very notions of right and wrong and of good and evil are often not the conventional ones.

14. They have an unhostile sense of humor. They do not consider funny what the average man considers funny, thus, they do not laugh at hostile humor.

15. They are highly creative. Each one shows in one way or another a special kind of creativeness, originality or inventiveness that has certain peculiar characteristics.

16. Resistance to enculturation. They get along with their culture but are not absorbed by it. In a certain profound and meaningful sense, they maintain an inner detachment from the traditions that they were raised with and the culture in which they are immersed.

17. They do not have a fear of the unknown. In fact they embrace it—simply becoming something to explore.

18. They are more objective (in every sense) than average people. This is true even when the problem concerns themselves, their own wishes, motives, hopes or aspirations.

19. They have the ability to concentrate and focus their attention to a degree not usual in the ordinary person.

20. They are autonomous, make their own decisions, are self-governing, and are active, responsible, self-disciplined, deciding agents rather than pawns, or helplessly *determined* by others. They make up their own minds, come to their own decisions, are self-starters, and are responsible for themselves and their own destinies.

21. The self-actualized person no longer *strives* in the ordinary sense. The motivation of ordinary men is to struggle for the basic need gratifications that they lack. But self-actualized people lack none

Maslow's Hierarchy of Needs

This chart depicts human needs from the most basic to the most refined.

of these gratifications. They work and are ambitious, even though in an unusual sense. For them, motivation is just a form of character growth.

22. The self-actualized count on blessings. They retain a sense of good fortune and show gratitude for what comes their way.

If you would like to know more about Maslow's findings from his extensive study of self-actualized people I would highly recommend reading his ground-breaking book, *Motivation and Personality*.

While working with, and closely studying self-actualized people, Abraham Maslow devised a way to look at and evaluate human needs *(see chart on page 41).* The ordinary person spends his/her time and energy in the pursuit of the fulfillment of these needs. On the foundation level we find the most urgent needs, which include food, shelter, clothing, etc. The next level relates to one's need for love and belonging. Everyone needs to feel appreciated, cared for, and a part of a family or group of people. The next level is about one's need for respect and self-esteem—the need to feel good about one's self—to know that you are valued and that you matter. Then comes the need for autonomy. Everyone wants to be in charge of his own life. We all want to feel capable and in control—self-governing.

The difference between the motivation of a self-actualized person and others lies in their perception of HOW life works.

The difference between the motivation of the self-actualized person and others lies in their perception of how life works. The self-actualized person understands that there are laws of nature, or principles of life, that are responsible for what happens in the material world of experience. If they live in harmony with these principles their needs and desires will be fulfilled. Other people do not have access to this knowledge and, therefore, have different beliefs about how to fulfill their needs. This lack of understanding creates stress, struggle and an unfulfilled life.

Self-actualization is about an inner state of being...a different WAY of knowing...accessing a deeper dimension of Self.

Self-actualized people come in all different sizes, shapes and colors and their personalities are as varied as the rest of society. The things that distinguish them from others are rarely seen. Self-actualization is about an inner state of being. The self-actualized person has access to a different way of knowing.

"Know thyself" is advice that has been handed down by the wise throughout time. The self-actualized person knows himself in a way that has not been discovered by the majority of society. The self-actualized person has discovered another dimension of self. This could be considered the spiritual dimension of one's self. It has nothing to do with religion—it is the experience of knowing one's self on a totally different level than is available to the five senses and the intellect.

People living in what I call a *three-dimensional world* have only the five physical senses and the intellect to use as tools of perception. In this state we can never see the big picture because the senses and the intellect are limited. They are only capable of seeing parts of the whole.

This reminds me of a story I once heard about a group of men who were looking at an elephant through holes in a wooden fence. One man who saw only the elephant's leg said the elephant was like a tree. Another, seeing only the body, described the elephant as a gray wall. One who saw only the tusk, thought the elephant was a marble pillar. Yet another, seeing only the tail, described it as a curly snake. None of them could know what the elephant looked like, since they could only see part of him.

The same thing is true for us when we have only the senses and the intellect for perceiving the nature of life. This is why we make poor choices and create much of the unpleasantness in our lives. It is like trying to put together a puzzle with most of the pieces missing.

Although self-actualized people are highly unique individuals, they share some basic attributes in common—knowing themselves on a deep level, ensuring that their own needs are being met, being aware of the Oneness of life, being open to infinite possibilities, taking full responsibility for their lives, being conscious of their choice and always observing their experiences. These aspects of LIVING are all more about BEING rather than DOING.

The self-actualized person has access to the wholeness of life. He has all the puzzle pieces he needs. Along the way, he has developed another very important tool to use for perception which we call intuition. Intuitive awareness comes from a level of wholeness. From this level we can see not only all the parts, but also how they fit together. Consequently, the self-actualized person sees life from a totally different perspective and has the ability to function in a much more effective manner.

The self-actualized person perceives the nature of life. He sees the perfection in all of creation, and becomes aware of the laws of nature that govern the material world, and our life experiences. When one becomes aware of these principles, it becomes clear how to work with them to create the life one wants.

Self-actualization is a human potential. It is something we can all grow into and experience for ourselves. In order to do this we must make some changes in our lives. It has been said that *"nothing changes until you do."* Our first choice is to take some time to prioritize our lives. Spend some quiet time contemplating the possibilities. Take walks out in nature and spend some *quality time* with your thoughts and feelings.

The state of self-actualization is a human potential. It is something we can all grow into and experience for ourselves.

Our next choice must be to focus our attention on the creation of optimal health. Remember, the state of our nervous system determines how efficiently the mind and the body function together. We need a strong nervous system to begin the journey towards self-actualization. *Part Three* of this book provides step-by-step guidelines for creating optimal health, which includes the growth and development of self-actualization. The process described and the exercises provided will produce a state of being that prepares people to take charge of their lives and create whatever they choose.

5

Five Laws of Nature that Govern Our Lives

All that a man has externally in multicapacity is intrinsically One. Here all the blades of grass, wood and stone, all things are One. This is the deepest depth and thereby am I completely captivated.

—Meister Eckhart,
thirteenth century German philosopher

Laws of nature are unchanging principles that determine our experiences—principles that govern how life works. These laws are unseen, but impact everything around us. In order to appreciate how life works, we need to understand at least some of these laws. Here are seven laws of nature that will help us comprehend the role we each play in creating our own experiences. The first law is:

ONE — *Everything in existence is Love expressing intelligently through Energy*

I use the word *Love* to identify the *Source of Creation*. Whether we look at it from a scientific or theological perspective, the result is the same. Where I use the term *Love*, a theologian would use the word *God*—a physicist might use the term *Unified Field*. The *Source* has been referred to by numerous names in sacred writings throughout the world. Most of us use the name *God*, but there are many synonyms for *God—Love, Light, Principle, Life, Mind* or *Spirit*. I use the word *Love* because this book is about learning how to experience *our* Source, and I believe our experience of Love, and the power of Love, best brings us to this experience.

Einstein's unified field theory states that everything in existence originates from and returns to the same source. Therefore, everything is an expression of Source and all intelligence is contained within it. The Source (Love) creates all of creation as an expression of itself. Imagine a large circle with a dot in the center. Let the circumference of the circle represent all of creation, and let the dot represent the Source. In order to express itself the Source moves in an intelligent way which creates all energy.

Einstein's theory of relativity tells us that everything in existence is energy. Energy can be either *gross* or *refined*. A rock is gross or dense energy, the human body is a more refined energy, and the mind is even more highly refined. What appears to be matter is just energy vibrating at a very rapid rate. Scientists tell us that the physical world is made up of tiny particles of matter moving at unimaginable speeds within empty space. Guided by intelligence and governed by the laws of nature, energy becomes form. Gross energy manifests within the density of the *physical world*. The more refined energies of thoughts and desires manifest in the *mental world*. These two *worlds* are intimately connected. All of this energy is intelligent and invincible. Energy is never destroyed, it only changes form. When we can understand this, we will begin to see how *creation is created,* and our role in it.

When asked *"Who are you?"* most people would say that they are a doctor, attorney, executive, secretary or a mother, wife, husband, or father. Maybe they would identify themselves by their religion or philosophy. This, however, is not who we *are*. It's what we do and how we relate to other people in the world around us. When you take away these kinds of identification, then who are you, *really?*

Hopefully you can see that you do not exist as a separate entity. We are each whole and complete within ourselves, but at the same time, we exist in relationship to others. On the spiritual level we are *Love (the Source),* on the mental level we are *Intelligence* and on the physical level we are *Energy*. We are all connected to Universal Intelligence and made out of the same material. Everything in existence is connected. We and other expressions in the universe are only separate in form.

The next question then is: *"How do forms come into being?"* This leads us to the second law of nature we want to explore:

TWO — *Thought directs energy*

From ancient science we find that Heraclitus (535 – 475 B.C.) states, *"The universe is generated not according to time, but according to thought."* In modern science we find

Sir James Jeans (1877–1946) who states, *"The universe begins to look more like a great thought than a great machine."* Sir Arthur Eddington, a British physicist, puts it this way: *"The stuff of the world is mind stuff."*

Thought creates movement. Therefore, we could say that when Love (the Source) thinks—creation occurs. It is the thought, the intent or belief of the thinker, that directs energy or attracts the energy necessary to manifest a particular thought or belief. As expressions of the Source (Love), we also create our world of experiences in the same way. We could say that spiritual energy directs mental energy, which in turn directs physical energy. Consequently, what we experience is a result of our thoughts. The next law of nature that comes into play here is:

THREE — *The law of attraction and repulsion*

Our attention, thoughts and deepest beliefs work together to create forms. The law of attraction and repulsion acts like a vacuum to pull in the energy necessary to fill these forms. Energy is always readily available for creating anything, but what we experience will be whatever we *truly* believe in and are focusing our attention on. The law of attraction and repulsion works both ways. This law repels the energy that does not fit the form created by our thoughts, beliefs and attention.

We could say that spiritual energy directs mental energy, which in turn directs physical energy. Consequently, what we experience is a result of our thoughts.

You have heard the statement, *"What comes from us returns to us, or what goes around comes around."* This is due to the law of attraction and repulsion. It works like a boomerang. The energy that we create through our thoughts goes out into the energy fields and attracts to itself its perfect reflection, and returns it to us. Anything is possible, but only what we believe in will be our experience.

This brings us to the next law we want to explore, which is:

FOUR — *Giving and Receiving are two sides of the same coin*

You can't have one without the other. If someone wants to give you a gift, but you say, *"I can't take that from you,"* nothing happens, right?

The energy that we generate through our thoughts and feelings go out into the energy fields and attracts to itself its perfect reflection, and returns it to us.

Most of us think that we would certainly accept whatever we want if it were given to us, but the truth is that most of us do not know how to receive. Since we now know that everything is energy and readily available for forming into whatever we want, we can see that anything and everything is being offered to us. Why aren't we accepting it? Because we have not understood the nature of energy, and how it works. Another law of nature, which fits in here, is:

FIVE — *Everything in the relative world is always changing*

Energy—the building blocks of everything in creation—is always in motion. Energy freely moves from one form to another. It flows in and out of everything and builds whatever form is appropriate. For example, Dr. Deepak Chopra tells us that the body is always in a process of renewing itself. At a recent lecture I attended, he said that the body we came into his lecture with would not the body that we would be going home in. During the course of the lecture, *we* would change. Energy is constantly moving in and out of the body, re-creating all the cells within itself.

The energy of the universe flows in and out in the same manner in which we breathe, constantly changing from one form to another. We bring energy into our bodies in the form of oxygen that regenerates our cells. We *receive* the energy. Then we breathe out the energy in the form of carbon dioxide. We *return* the energy. This energy now exists in a form beneficial to help nourish the plants in our environment. Plants continue the cycle. They breathe out oxygen in response to the carbon dioxide we provide. This flow must continue in order to create healthy bodies for *both* humans and plants. If we try to hold on to the air, it doesn't work. The same is true for everything—we must receive *and* give—to keep the flow of energy working in our lives trusting that the energy will change form to benefit all involved. We will discuss this further and see how it works in other areas of our lives. The next law of nature is:

The energy of the universe flows in and out. The energy in our creations also needs to flow in the same way.

SIX — *Beliefs are simply information that we have accepted as truth.*

We become very attached to our beliefs because we think they are *absolutely* true and unchanging. What actually happens, however, is that since our thoughts and beliefs *create* our experiences, we simply witness a demonstration of our core beliefs manifesting the same experience over and over again. The effect is that these foundation beliefs continue to be validated.

Until we open to accepting, allowing and receiving energy, reality creation can be a challenge.

Beliefs are just thoughts and feelings about how life works that have been programmed in the subconscious mind. We have a belief which manifests and validates the belief. This creates the closed-circuit cycle that keeps us believing and manifesting the same things. We become aware of our limiting beliefs as we grow. At one time, a certain belief may have benefited us, but as we expand our experiences, they can hold us back. It is important to note—all beliefs continue to function until we consciously change them.

Most of the beliefs we hold have been handed down to us from our parents, friends and our culture. Few of us have ever questioned them. As children we learn how to manage in the world by observing our parents and the people around us. These authority figures teach us *their* beliefs over and over again, and through repetition, we accept them as truth. Unless we stop and question these beliefs, they keep running our lives. We will continue creating the things that our family and culture believes in until we decide to choose our *own* beliefs.

Our beliefs form the energy templates that creates our experiences. It is important to remember that we are free to change what we believe whenever we choose.

When we begin to investigate, we soon see that what we believed to be true at one time turns out not to be true later on. For many years people believed the earth was flat, and that was the collective experience. We see the same phenomenon in reports from scientists in the medical arena. Something that is first believed to be of great benefit to our health turns out to actually be damaging. Everything we have accepted as truth in the relative world is always changing. The only absolute, non-changing truths are the laws of nature.

In our lives, we are always experiencing the results of the choices we've made. Make new choices—create new experiences.

Our beliefs form the energy that creates our experiences, but we are free to believe whatever we choose. Once we clearly understand that our beliefs are creating our experiences, we can see how important it is to bring as many of our beliefs to our consciousness as possible and evaluate them. Once we know that they are not necessarily true, we also know that we have a choice about what we want to do with them.

This brings us to the seventh law of nature, which is:

SEVEN — *We all make our own choices*

Other people may coerce us, threaten us, or present us with numerous ideas for our consideration, but ultimately we must choose. Even when we choose not to choose, we have still made a choice. This choice is to give someone else the power to make our decisions for us, but it is still a choice. We, ourselves, give the power to other people and situations to control our lives.

This is a principle that many of us are not aware of, but when we look into it, we realize that it is a fact of life. We experience the results of the choices we have made. We may not realize we have options, but that again is a belief which we can change. We always have options, even though we may not be able to see them at any given time.

Once we accept the fact that we make our own choices, we are able to take our own power back, even if we have given it away to beliefs that do not serve us well. Many times we hear ourselves make the statement *"I* have *to* ____________________ *(fill in the blank)."* When we catch ourselves making such a statement, it is very helpful to change it to *"I am* choosing *to."* This makes us aware of the fact that we have options, and we are, indeed, in charge of our choices, and will experience the consequences of them.

We will look at more examples of how these principles of life are working in our experiences as we continue on.

6 Six

Why Are We NOT Self-Actualized?

Consciousness is a source of self-cognition quite apart from and independent of reason. Through his reason man observes himself, but only through consciousness does he know himself.

—Leo Tolstoy

Self-actualization is our natural state. Why, then, are we not *ALL* self-actualized? What blocks this natural ability from our awareness?

Levels of Consciousness

There are many states of consciousness, but here we need only look at and understand the three major states.

1. *Conscious-awareness.* This is the state you are in as you read this book. We could describe the conscious mind as *present awareness.* It is the level of thinking, discrimination, choice, reason and logic.
2. *The Subconscious.* It is very powerful, but cannot discriminate or choose—it simply stores data. All the information taken in through the senses is stored in the subconscious. Much information goes into the subconscious that we are not *consciously* aware of. Many of our beliefs have never existed on the conscious level —we never made a conscious choice about them. Our beliefs come from this "storehouse" of information. Then, we use these beliefs to create our experiences.
3. *The Superconscious.* This is the level of *ALL* intelligence—*ALL* knowledge. We access the superconscious on a deep level of silence. Here, we connect with all knowledge—*intuitive awareness.* It is a part of who we are, but we usually are not aware of it. ***Everything in existence is Love expressing intelligently through Energy.*** The superconscious is what we could call *Universal Intelligence.* The reason we are unable to access it is due to the energy aspect of who we are. Earlier we talked about how energy expresses itself in different levels of density. A rock is a very dense form of energy while

the body and mind is more refined. The superconscious is the most highly refined form of energy. In order for us to access it, our mind/body energy must become more highly refined.

Energy

If we are observant, we can see and feel the energy movement in our lives. Notice the "heaviness" when someone around you is being very negative, making statements about how bad things are, and predicting that they are going to get worse. The energy of everything in the surrounding environment becomes more dense. Then, notice how you feel when you are in the presence of someone who is upbeat and positive. There is a feeling of lightness. Their optimistic attitude allows the surrounding energy to become more refined. Better yet, notice the energy within yourself when you are thinking negative and positive thoughts. You will be able to feel the difference. Another good test is to observe the energy in your body when you get into an argument or encounter some form of conflict. You can feel the energy contract, becoming strained and uncomfortable. You can see how this kind of energy, or stress, can create disease and malfunctions in the body. Most doctors agree that at least ninety-eight percent of all illness is stress-related. Let's look at how stress affects our ability to become self-actualized.

The information stored in the subconscious is used to create our beliefs and then these beliefs are used to create our experiences.

We access the superconscious at the level of silence we reach through meditation. Knowledge gained from this level is what we call intuitive awareness.

Stress

Hans Selye, who dedicated his life to the study of stress, defines it as *any demand made on the body*. He speaks of two kinds of stress which he calls eustress and distress.

Eustress is created by the positive, exciting experiences in our lives—distress is produced by negative thoughts and pressures. Since we describe stress as *any demand made on the body,* we can see that positive *and* negative experiences will both burden the nervous system. Whether positive or negative—it still means more work for the system. Our nervous system is responsible for carrying messages from the senses to the brain and dispatching the brain's response to all parts of the body. Anytime we burden our nervous system, we are impacting how effectively it does its job.

Stress is described as any demand made on the mind/body system. Positive and negative experiences BOTH create additional work for the nervous system.

A certain amount of stress is essential to life. Problems arise when there are more demands made on the mind/body system than it can handle. Most of the time we are not even aware that we are over-stressed, because the nervous system is also responsible for our perception. We usually think we are fine until something happens to us and we burst into tears or yell at someone over something small. Uncontrollable laughter is also a sign that the nervous system is over-stressed. When the system becomes overloaded it begins to malfunction. Have you noticed when you are over-stressed that you are also unable to see possibilities? When stress levels are high, it is almost impossible to find solutions to the problems we face. If the stress is not too severe, after we get a good night's sleep, things look different. The period of rest has given the nervous system an opportunity to heal itself and return to its normal functioning.

If we choose to become self-actualized, we must create a lifestyle that reduces stress and strengthens the nervous system on a daily basis.

Unfortunately, a severely over-stressed nervous system is the reality most of us have created for ourselves. We usually start over-stressing when we are children. It builds even stronger during our adolescent years. For most people, stress has been accumulating ever since those years. Every day, building on the next, stress continues to pile up. So much so that even a full night of sleep has little effect. ***As the system becomes more and more stressed, the mind/body energy becomes less refined, and more dense.*** This is the main reason why we are not all self-actualized. The stress that builds up in our nervous systems over the years is what blocks our ability to connect with the superconscious on a conscious level. As we stated before, the superconscious is the most refined energy possible, and the mind/body energy must become more refined in order to be capable of experiencing it.

The main reason most of us are not already self-actualized is that the stored up stress makes us unable to access the highly-refined energy of the superconscious.

If we choose to become self-actualized, we must create a lifestyle that reduces stress and strengthens the nervous system on a daily basis. In *Part Three* of this book I have laid out a routine that, if practiced daily, will help you do just that. This process, when practiced over time, will refine the energy of the mind/body system, thereby making the system capable of merging with the superconscious.

When the energy of the mind/body system is sufficiently refined, it automatically merges with the superconscious and we begin to know and understand the laws of nature and how life really works. This experience is like moving into a new world—a place of joy, bliss and understanding—a *way of being* where we intuitively know whatever we need to know to create the life we want. This is life in a completely different dimension from what we experience when we live in the world of the conscious and subconscious mind alone.

There is also another major factor that blocks our path to self-actualization. Let's take a look at it.

Beliefs

We are born into this world totally dependent upon other people to care for us and teach us how to survive and manage. At this time we have no conscious awareness of how anything works. We learn from others, and what they teach us is their beliefs. They provide us the best information they have, but they simply pass on the beliefs of those who raised them. We are so busy trying to learn how to fulfill our needs that we seldom stop to question the information that we are given. Consequently, the same information gets handed down from generation to generation. It is not until we stop and question the validity of this information that we discover that it might not be accurate at all—there might be a better way.

For the most part, we are working off of the belief systems of others. Without meaning to, we have fully accepted the opinions of others to guide the course of events in our lives.

I heard a story once about a woman who always cut off the end of her roast before cooking it. One day her daughter asked her why she did this. The woman explained that it was just how you cook a roast. She had always done it that way. Her mother had taught her how to cook, and that was what she knew. She had never even thought about it before, but it did make her a bit curious. So she called her own mother and asked her the same question. It had nothing to do with cooking a better roast. Her mother cut the end off of the roast simply because her pan wasn't big enough to hold the entire roast. This is an example of how something that worked for one person could be totally inappropriate for another, yet we keep carrying it forward.

If you desire to create the life you're dreaming of, it is time to become more aware of your beliefs and change the ones that don't serve you.

Most of us believe many things that do not help us in creating what we want in our lives. We, of course, are convinced that our beliefs are correct, because they are so deeply linked to our experiences. Since most of our beliefs have been programmed into our subconscious without being aware of them, we never had a chance to question them at all. But now that we know that these beliefs are creating our experiences, it is time to start exploring them more consciously.

There is always a dialogue going on in our minds. For people who are not self-actualized, this dialogue is between the conscious and the subconscious mind. When we think about something consciously, the subconscious begins to tell the conscious mind about all the information it already has on the subject. Since it is the job of the subconscious to simply record and store everything it comes into contact with, it has gathered a lot of conflicting information. The conscious mind tries to sort through all this information trying to come up with what it thinks is a reasonable conclusion. What we do not realize is that much the information on which we have to make our decisions is somewhat arbitrary. Since we are used to receiving information from outside sources, we think it is the only way to get information. No one ever tells us that we are connected to universal intelligence, and can access all knowledge right within ourselves. The reason for this, of course, is because most of the world is invested in a system where we look outside ourselves for *correct information*. Whether we seek out the *perceived experts*, authority figures, religion, science, history—it rarely occurs to us that much of this information is *not* going to be helpful. We continue to live our lives the same way, over and over again, because of the ineffective and limiting beliefs we hold on to, and the stress that makes it impossible for the conscious mind to communicate with the superconscious.

Every belief is simply someone's opinion. Your opinion is just as good as anyone else's. The question is "does this opinion help me create what I am wanting to experience, or not"?

We all have our *own* personal beliefs which create our *own* experiences. Then there are cultural beliefs which most of us buy into. Add to this—religious beliefs, scientific assumptions, family rituals, societal understandings—and we begin to realize that very little of it relates to who we really are. Since our information comes from others, we believe that if a large number of people believe something, then it must be true. Again, we accept it without question.

Let's go back and take another look at a couple of the laws of nature that are governing our lives. Law #5 is ***Everything in the relative world is always changing,*** and Law #6 is ***Beliefs are simply information that we have accepted as truth.*** Since everything is always changing, even if what we were taught to believe actually was truth, most of it is probably now obsolete. Then, as we realize that ***beliefs are just information that we have accepted as truth,*** we can see that relative truth is also always changing. Law #7 is ***We all make our own choices.*** In light of this, we can see that many of the things we believe are not of benefit to us. Not only *can* we change them, but we *must.*

Every belief is simply someone's opinion. Your opinion is just as good as anyone else's. The question is *"does this opinion help me create what I am wanting to experience, or not"?*

Once we understand what buying into other people's beliefs has created for us, we find the motivation to make different choices. If we want to become self-actualized, and create unlimited futures for ourselves, we will need to change many of our beliefs.

Some people have a hard time believing that THEY can function from a more advanced level. This belief MUST change before you can even begin.

Some people have a hard time believing that anyone can function from a more advanced level, and certainly not them. This, of course, is one of the foundation beliefs that needs to be changed. If you reach a place where you begin to believe that self-actualization is actually possible, but that it won't happen to you—it will feel like pressing your nose against the glass yearning to get inside. All that keeps you outside is a belief—your belief.

In *Part Three,* we will discuss how we become aware of our beliefs and how to change them. Next, let's look at how we actually create our experiences.

Seven

How We Create Our Own Experiences

There is an inmost center in us all,
where truth abides in fullness.

—Robert Browning, nineteenth century poet

Let's go back to our example of how *creation is created.* Remember, we used an example of a circle with a dot in the center. The dot represented the *source* of creation, and the circle represented *what* is created. When the source thinks (moves), energy is created. Everything is made up of this energy.

My husband has a doctorate in theology, and has discovered that all the principles in this book have been written about in sacred writings throughout history. However, for the most part, we have completely missed them. He frequently refers to the Bible for help to explain the principle of how creation is *created.* The Bible says that we are all created in the image and likeness of God. Just as God, or whatever you call the source, created all of creation, we, in the same manner, create our *own personal worlds.*

When the Source thinks (moves), energy is created. Everything in our lives originates from the thoughts projected from that single point.

Imagine yourself being the dot in the center of your world. When you think, your thoughts direct energy. This energy is subject to ***the law of attraction and repulsion*** and goes out into the energy fields attracting to itself whatever form is appropriate to manifest that particular thought.

This is the basic principle, but it isn't quite so simple. Both the conscious and subconscious minds play significant roles in manifesting our creations. A thought is a conscious act. It is formed in the subconscious. Remember, the subconscious stores *all* of the information it has *ever* received. Since it cannot make judgments, it only knows what is important and what is not by the charge of the energy imprinted on the thought. We hold a lot of conflicting information and whatever is charged with the most emotion comes up first. The conscious mind sifts through all this information and thinks thoughts that are formed by our deepest beliefs. It is not an instantaneous thing. Consequently, every thought doesn't manifest immediately.

If our thoughts were to manifest instantaneously we might see something like this. You think: "OK, if I can create whatever I want, I want a new Mercedes." Bingo, you get it. Actually, you would have to think, "I have created a new Mercedes". If you thought, "I want a Mercedes" you would, indeed, create the experience of *wanting* a Mercedes. Then you think, "I have now created a new mansion for myself—twenty-four rooms, built-in swimming pool, etc." You get it. Then you decide to create twenty million dollars in your bank account. Bingo, you get it. Then you think, "Wow, this is too good to be true!" Swish, away it all goes.

Fortunately, it doesn't work this way. When you have a conscious thought, the subconscious checks its files to let you know if the thought coincides with the information in its data banks. If it doesn't, you will most likely change the thought to be in harmony with the information stored in the subconscious, to be consistent with your beliefs. Here on the conscious level you could choose to change the underlying beliefs, but it requires significant strength and determination. We will look at how we do this in upcoming chapters. Most of the time, we do not deliberately generate our thoughts. They spontaneously come to the conscious mind via the subconscious, automatically in sync with our beliefs.

This is one of the main reasons we are unable to understand how our beliefs create our experiences. We are out-of-touch with many of our beliefs and have very little awareness of where our thoughts and feelings come from. They often seem to come out of nowhere as an instinctive reaction to the things going on in the world around us. It's challenging enough to comprehend that our *inner* beliefs and *outer* experiences are directly linked—never mind that one actually *causes* the other. The intellect (the conscious and subconscious mind) is not capable of following this cause-and-effect relationship for the time

Most of the time, we do not deliberately generate our thoughts—they automatically rise up from our subconscious mind. It is helpful to start paying attention to the thoughts we habitually think.

necessary for its completion. It does not work in straight-line time, which is all the intellect understands.

We can, however, begin to see how this principle works by observing the thought patterns and experiences of others around us. In time we will be able to see it in ourselves, but it is easier by beginning to observe it in others. This way we do not yet have to deal with the rationale of our own thinking.

We can begin to have a stronger connection with our beliefs by observing how they demonstrate themselves in the experiences of our life.

People talk about the things they believe, and many times you will hear them say the same kinds of things over and over. An example would be: "I just can't seem to get ahead no matter what I do." You can observe their beliefs demonstrating themselves in their lives. You will notice that even when this person gets some extra money from some unexpected source, something always happens to use it up. Their car will break down or the washing machine will go on the fritz. Whatever we believe on the deepest level of the subconscious will become true for us. In one of our classes, it was interesting to observe from a discussion, how our beliefs differ and produce the *believed-in* result. One participant was talking about his health problems, then others joined in to discuss their health issues. Then another person said, *"I can't relate to what you are talking about. I have never been sick a day in my life."* Then he added, *"But I sure have a hard time making any money."* The one with health problems replied, *"Making money is very easy for me, but I am sick a lot."* When we start observing, it is easy to see how people create an experience of their beliefs.

Let's look at how cultural beliefs work. Back in the fourteenth century, almost everyone believed that the world was flat. Then, Christopher Columbus had an intuitive awareness. It came to him that the world was actually round. Everyone said he was crazy. They all knew that the earth was flat, and that if you went too far out you would fall off. But as we know, he persuaded Queen Isabella to give him a fleet of ships so he could test his idea. His expedition proved that his intuitive inspiration was correct. What do you think his friends said when he returned? Did they say, "Bravo, Columbus, you proved us wrong," or did they say, "That can't be right." After all, these were intelligent people. They had attended universities, and all the professors taught them that the world was flat. Would they give up their cherished beliefs that easily? Probably not. If Columbus had persuaded them to sail around the world with him, they would have experienced for themselves the fact that the world was round. However, they still lived in a world where everyone else believed that it was flat. They would have lost their personal fear, but still be part of a society that *lived in fear* of falling off the earth.

Self-actualized people have figuratively sailed around the world. They know that life doesn't work the way most people believe it does. They have lost their fear of the unpredictable. They understand the laws of nature and how we each individually create our own experiences.

Self-actualized people are pioneers and explorers who have developed an intimate relationship with their intuitive minds. Because of this, they demonstrate a high level of personal confidence and have lost their fear of the unpredictable.

All new ideas come from the superconscious, intuitively. The subconscious can only give us information that has been programmed into it. Every new discovery, every new invention, and what we call genius, all come to us as an intuitive inspiration from the superconscious. The superconscious is available to anyone who makes a choice to release the stress stored in the nervous system and merges with their true self. It is a matter of taking the time and doing whatever is necessary to become capable of discovering the personal resources deep within.

When we make a choice to heal the mind/body system, to take charge of our lives and change our beliefs, we will discover that we are indeed ***Love expressing***

ourselves intelligently through energy. It is the stress stored in the system that also blocks our awareness of the Love. As the stress is released and the system gets stronger, we begin to experience Love on a very different level. We will know Love as the source of all creation, and the power of the universe—we are all a perfect expression of Love, Intelligence and Energy.

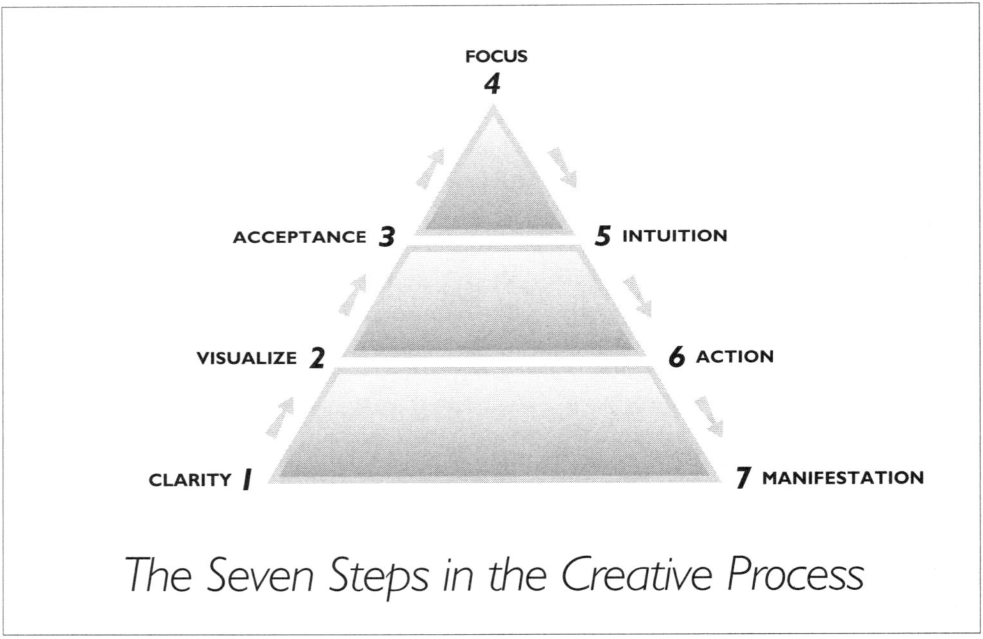

The Seven Steps in the Creative Process

There is a process to use for creating whatever we want in our lives. Here is a brief overview of the steps involved. In *Part Three,* we will work through this process in more detail.

Step 1 is Clarity

The first thing we need to establish is what we want. For many people it takes some time to get clear on exactly what they desire. We *will* create whatever we focus our attention on, so we want to be sure about it. Most of us have spent the majority of our lives simply reacting to what happens to us. Now that we understand we are creating whatever we experience, it is time to start creating *consciously*. If we do not get clear on what we want, we will continue to create whatever the subconscious believes in.

Step 2 is Visualization

Sometimes people tell me that they do not know how to visualize. They are mistaken. They just do not recognize that they already DO visualize—we all do it all the time. For example: if I say to you, "Do not picture a pink cow in your mind," what happens? You visualize a pink cow. Visualization is a part of imagination. You can't *keep* from doing it.

A visual image creates a form in mind. This form attracts the energy necessary to fill it. When this process is completed, whatever we are visualizing manifests in the material world. Of course, everything we visualize does not manifest. Some additional energies are necessary for manifestation, which brings us to the next step.

Step 3 is Acceptance

Acceptance is the most difficult step for most people. You might be thinking, "*Why wouldn't I accept what I want?*" This is where our beliefs come in. Remember that about eighty-five percent of what we believe is not on the conscious level. Therefore, we are out-of-touch with most of our beliefs. In order to work through the acceptance step, we *must* become conscious of our beliefs. If our beliefs do not support our visions, we must change them to be in alignment with what we want to create. Our visions cannot be manifested in the material world until we first have accepted them in our minds. Energy is formed on the mental level before it manifests on the physical level.

Step 4 is Focusing Attention

Whatever we focus our attention on is what we attract into our lives.

- ***We need to be CLEAR about what we want to create.*** We tend to focus our attention on our problems, thus creating more problems. *Focusing our attention on something automatically attracts the energy that MATCHES whatever we are focusing on.* Experiences must have energy to exist and they get the energy from the attention we focus on them. If we believe we have a problem and focus our attention on it, we attract the energy to perpetuate the problem. The best way to alleviate a problem is to stop giving it attention. It will go away. It is critically important for us to learn to *focus our attention on what we want* instead of on our problems.
- ***The second area is our ABILITY to focus.*** When the nervous system is over-stressed, it becomes increasingly difficult to direct our focus on what we want. *It invariably wanders off onto our problems, or is distracted by fear and doubt.* As the system becomes stronger, our perception clears, and we are able to see possibilities. Fear and doubt fade away. Once we are strong enough to focus our attention on what we want in more powerful ways, things start to happen much faster. *Focus* is the capstone on our chart of the Seven Steps in the Creative Process *(see page 66)*. Once we focus on what we want to create, the remainder of the process is downhill.

Step 5 is Intuitive Inspiration

Once the nervous system releases a sufficient amount of stress, the mind/body energy becomes more refined, automatically putting us in touch with intuitive awareness. Intuitive inspiration is always available to us, but much of the time we are not capable of tuning in to it. When our energy has become sufficiently refined so that it can vibrate in harmony with the superconscious, the only thing we have to do is listen. Intuitive inspiration is always there for us when we listen for its guidance.

The way we learn to listen to our intuition is by stilling the intellect. We must teach the *thinking aspect of our minds* to settle down. Our thoughts are constantly moving, and our minds are so active that we cannot hear our intuition as long as these thoughts are demanding all our attention. In order to tap into intuitive awareness, we teach the *conscious mind* how to focus. Once focused, it settles down and automatically merges with the superconscious. *This is the level of all knowledge.* Each time we merge the conscious mind with the superconscious, we return with expanded awareness. This is how we open the path for intuitive insights to flow into the conscious mind.

This process is called meditation. When we meditate on a regular basis, we open the channel for intuitive inspiration to flow into the conscious mind whenever it is needed. When we have a question, we simply ask. We go into meditation, and the answer will soon appear. The response appears in many different ways. Once we learn that the answers will come and we begin to expect them, this process becomes quite automatic. We will work with specific techniques for preparing ourselves to be capable of receiving intuitive guidance in *Part Three.* The fifth step is to listen to our intuitive inspiration for what we need to do to manifest our vision.

Step 6 is Action

This part is easy when we have worked through the first five steps. We simply follow through with whatever comes to us through our intuitive guidance. This action step cannot be overlooked. Since it is closest to the manifestation step, we think it is the most important. Action—without the other five steps in preparation for it—is usually ineffective. Often, we go from a vague idea of what we want right into action. If we work hard enough, and long enough, we will get some results, but they may not be what we intended. Even when we are fortunate enough to create our desire using this method, it is the hard way to go.

Step 7 is Manifestation

After we complete the first six steps, manifestation is inevitable. It is difficult to even see this as a separate step, but it is important to recognize it as a part of the process. By the time we have created what we wanted, we can easily overlook the fact that we, ourselves, created it. If we are aware and observe the entire process, it becomes much easier to understand exactly how we *bring things into being,* and how we can create whatever we want.

Meditation

There is another important discipline that we want to touch upon here that plays a major role in understanding how we can create our visions in the fastest and most effective way possible—meditation.

In *Part Three,* I will give you some guidelines for learning how to meditate, but here I want you to know how it works in manifesting our visions.

Meditation is a process that is accomplished by bringing the body and mind to a point of stillness and silence. When we accomplish this, the conscious mind merges with the superconscious, which is all intelligence. This is the level of all possibilities. This is what we call universal intelligence, an aspect of the source. This is the level where all of creation begins. On the level of the source, energy has not yet been formed. However, the most powerful thoughts we can have for manifesting our desires are as close as possible to this level. Once the Source moves (thinks), energy is created. We can give form to this energy by bringing into our consciousness whatever we want to create. In *Part Three,* we will have specific guidelines for how to do this.

Eight 8

It's All About Choice

Destiny is not a matter of chance,
it is a matter of choice—it is not a thing to
be waited for, it is a thing to be achieved.

—William Jennings Bryan

The seventh law of nature, discussed in *chapter 5,* states:

SEVEN — *We all make our own choices*

We make choices that coincide with our beliefs. Every choice has a consequence—that is how our experiences come to be. Even if we *choose not to choose,* we have *still* made a choice, and we will *still* experience the consequence of that choice.

This law of nature guarantees us the power to take charge of our lives and create them any way we choose. Many times we cannot see a choice that we believe will bring about our desired result. In this case, we usually say, *"I have no choice."* Since we are an expression of universal intelligence, we always have choices. There are infinite choices possible, but we may not be able to see them at any given time. The two things that block our ability to see possibilities are—first, the stress that keeps the nervous system from functioning as it was designed to function and, second, our deep-seated beliefs.

Whenever we have problems seeing the full range of possibilities in front of us—look to releasing stress and working with our limited beliefs to open up our perspective.

When we find ourselves in a situation where we cannot see any possibilities that would fulfill our desires, we need to get some rest, do the program that is provided in *Part Three,* and question our beliefs. Anything is possible, but it is our beliefs that limit us. Again, we need to remember that ***beliefs are just information that we have accepted as true.*** When we are able to see our beliefs from a different perspective, we begin to realize that they are not necessarily true, and that we can change them.

Since the seven laws of nature are governing our lives, we are all born with the innate ability to create the life we want for ourselves. The reason we are unaware of this is because we do not know who we are. When we choose to follow the program laid out in *Part Three* on a daily basis, we begin to discover who we really are. With practice, over time, we come to know that we are *at one with all power*. We are not separate entities, but we are *All Love, Intelligence and Energy*. There is nothing else in existence, therefore nothing is separate from us.

We discover that our desires and the fulfillment of our desires come from the same source. There is nothing wrong with our desires. The problems arise from the *means* we use to fulfill them. These difficulties are a result of either our *inability* to fulfill our desires, or our *lack of understanding*. All we need do is bring our conscious awareness to the level of the Source, which contains all intelligence, and we can intuitively know how to make choices that will produce the desired result.

Our desires and the fulfillment of our desires come from the same source. There is nothing wrong with our desires. The problems arise from the means we use to fulfill them.

Let's look at why we do not know the power that lies dormant within each of us. Our physical bodies, including our nervous systems, are capable of handling only a limited amount of stress. Here's an example explaining what happens when the system can no longer function properly, and the stress keeps coming.

It is a stressful experience to be a child. They are trying to learn how the world works and where they fit into it. Since they are only beginning to develop and have a limited ability to understand, children can be very cruel. I will never forget an incident that I experienced in grade school. I was returning to class from recess when I came upon a group of fifteen or twenty children who had cornered a little girl and were verbally assaulting her. The victim came from a very poor family. Her clothes were ragged, and she was not blessed with natural beauty. These children were calling her terrible names such as "scarecrow." My heart went out to her. I was enraged that they were treating her in such a manner, but did nothing about it. I simply walked by without saying anything. For years I felt guilty about not standing up for her, but I didn't—I couldn't. I did not believe that I could make a difference, and I was afraid that if I said anything they would start being nasty to me as well. My choice was one of self-preservation, but not an admirable one to me at the time.

Can you imagine the stress this situation caused this little girl? I am sure that this incident only added to the many other stressful pressures in her life. What happens when a child's or an adult's nervous system cannot handle it any more? They either have a nervous breakdown or they turn to violence. They can't help it—one or the other is inevitable or maybe both. Actually, becoming violent is a characteristic of a nervous system failure.

Many children learn to endure this kind of stress. Often, their poor self-image is due to the kind of family life they come from. The beliefs of those they are close to form the beliefs about themselves. Does this mean that this child, or any other child that survives abuse, is doomed to a life of misery? Absolutely not!

When a nervous system can handle no more stress people either have a nervous breakdown, turn to violence, or maybe BOTH.

All of us, no matter what age, have the power within ourselves to change our lives. It may not be easy, but anyone who reads this book can begin working with the process laid out in *Part Three,* and start releasing the stress that has been stored in the nervous system for so many years. Then they will discover their own inner power to create the kind of life they want. For most people, it is a process over time, but *everyone* can do it. The condition of our nervous system determines our ability to see possibilities and to make choices that work for us.

Let's now take a look at how energy affects us in our daily lives. Whatever we do, say, or believe is always putting out an energy. Due to the law of attraction and repulsion, this energy demands that *"like"* energy is returned. When someone smiles at us, we usually smile back, right? If someone is nasty to us, our natural reaction is to be nasty in return. However, we do have a choice. If we are strong enough to be conscious of what is happening, we can choose to react in a different manner. We could simply ask, *"What's wrong with you today?"* If we can move beyond the demand of the energy, and simply not buy into it, we can control how someone else's energy affects us.

How we feel or what we believe about ourselves is also constantly creating an energy field around us that demands that others respond in like manner. If we believe that we are ugly, stupid or useless, others will tend to believe it, too. On the other hand, since ***beliefs are simply information that we have accepted as true,*** we can choose to believe something quite different from what we have heard in the past. This, of course, requires a strong nervous system. If we are strong enough, and someone says to us, *"I think you are stupid!"* we can sidestep the energy, and say to ourself, *"I disagree. I think I am brilliant."* Most of these comments are not usually said out loud, but work purely on the level of thought. When we choose to release the stress stored in our nervous systems and create a strong positive self-image, we find people will respond to us with respect. Generally, other people will see us the way we see ourselves. It is an automatic and unconscious response.

How we feel or what we believe about ourselves is constantly creating an energy field around us that demands that others respond in like manner.

Let's look at my particular situation. I was fortunate to have a very loving family. My mother saw to it that I ate good nutritious food and everyone in my environment treated me well. I was mostly exposed to supportive beliefs, one of which was that I could accomplish whatever I chose to do. This background gave me a certain amount of confidence—enough to automatically receive the respect of the other children around me—but not enough to push my luck by defending someone who was not popular. Even under the best of circumstances, growing up in the world is stressful. We need to do everything possible to help our children feel good about themselves.

Many adults still carry the stress that was created while they were children. Think about your childhood and teen years. If these thoughts stir up an emotional reaction in you, then this stress is still stored in your nervous system. You can let it go through the practice of the process laid out in *Part Three,* and *consciously realize* that it is over. It doesn't matter any more and you can choose to let it go. After pursuing this for a while you can check your success by bringing the incident back to your consciousness and observing your feelings about it.

This brings us to another very important point that we need to understand. It is the other side of the principle that says, ***we all make our own choices.*** The law guarantees that we each enjoy the privilege of choosing for ourselves. It also infers that you cannot make choices for others. For example, we cannot change someone else. We can choose to have a happy, harmonious marriage, and we can even choose the characteristics of our partner. But, we cannot choose that a particular person fit a profile that we created, or make a certain individual want to be with us. When we are working with creating what we want, and we get clear about what the special person in our life will be like—it's like placing an order with Universal Intelligence. It will deliver whatever we ordered, but it will be a person who also wants someone like us. It could be someone we already know or someone entirely new to us. We all get to make our own choices, so we need to be sure that we understand this.

Not only are we allowed to make ALL our own choices—but it is important to realize that we can NOT make choices for others.

My husband, Dean, tells a story of a time when he was in the U.S. Navy. He and a black soldier, who was well-decorated for his contributions in the war, were boarding a bus somewhere in the South during a time when buses were segregated. The driver told the black soldier to go to the back of the bus, but there weren't any seats left in the black section. The driver said the soldier would have to get off. Dean told the driver that there was an empty seat next to him, and that the black soldier should be able to sit there. He demanded that the man should be able to stay on the bus. He explained what this black soldier had done for his country, and how he deserved to ride this bus if anyone did. Before he even knew what was happening, Dean found himself being taken from the bus and set out on the curb, the black soldier right beside him. The man looked over at Dean and asked, *"Where are you from, sir?"* and then explained that you just don't DO things like that down here.

Dean saw injustice and was strong enough to try to make a difference, which was admirable, but he was trying to make a choice for someone else. It didn't work. The principles of life provide us with a means for creating the life we want for ourselves, but no one else can do it for us. We can create our personal life the way we want it to be, but can we eliminate injustice? No. We can choose not to participate in it, but someone else has chosen to create it, which is simply a matter of the law working the way it works. We will all encounter obstacles on our path to accomplishing whatever we choose to do, whether it is taking a bus across town or other more important things. We then look at the situation and make a choice about how to handle it.

A friend of mine has written a book titled *A Woman Can Do That!* The book is a guide to help women overcome discrimination and achieve success in the workplace. She interviewed me along with a number of other women. One of the questions she asked me was how I handled the discrimination issue. I told her that my first choice was to avoid it whenever possible. This is an example of what you can do if a roadblock keeps showing up on your journey. My choice is always to simply go around it if possible.

After a very short career in the corporate world of bosses and employees, I realized that this was not the place for me. I needed to be an entrepreneur, and I have been one ever since. I still run into discrimination occasionally, but I simply ignore it.

When someone discriminates against woman—or anyone else for that matter—he is exercising his right to make choices. It is a *creation,* a *"gift"* someone wants to give me, but I am *NOT* accepting it. Remember the law of receiving, that ***giving and receiving are two sides of the same coin—you can't have one without the other.*** Consequently, if you refuse to receive something, nothing happens. Nothing can be given without a receiver, or received without a giver. This law also supports nature's perfect order of keeping each of us in charge of our own lives. We get to choose what we give—we get to choose what we receive.

The reason we have not discovered the power we have within ourselves is because we have always focused our attention outward.

Also remember, that a problem can only exist in our lives if we give it energy by focusing our attention on it. If we refuse to pay any attention to a problem, in time it will vanish. ***Everything in existence is energy,*** and we give energy to something by focusing our attention on it.

The reason we have not discovered the power we have within ourselves is because we have always focused our attention outward. We believe that others have all the power and that they can make life good or miserable for us. This belief, however, has not served us well. We are now discovering that all power is centered within us. This requires both a change in belief and a change in focus. When we want to do something good, it often means trying to change the world. So we go out there attempting to make choices for other people, and usually make little progress. If we want to change the world, we must start with ourselves. All of the power is right within us, but it only works to create whatever we want in *our* lives. However, if we see ourselves living in an orderly compassionate world, this vision puts out an energy that demands a *"like"* response.

Let's take a look now at how important it is for us to stay focused on our own self-interest. The universe is set up to function perfectly if we all do this. In fact, our own self-interest is really all we truly know. When we try to think of others before ourselves, this is a form of trying to make choices for other people. The system is perfect. We just need to understand how it works.

This reminds me of a time when I was single and living in an apartment building in Minneapolis. There was a really nice guy who also lived in my building. We saw each other at parties and talked a number of times. I knew he liked me and I was very impressed with him, too. At one of the building parties we discovered that we were both going to be in Chicago on business trips the following week. Neither of us knew anyone there, so we decided we would both stay for the weekend and enjoy the city together. I was really looking forward to my weekend date. Since I didn't know him well, I had no idea what kind of things he liked to do, so I decided to let him choose our activities for us. He also was determined to make a good impression with me, so he made the same decision. The weekend was a disaster. He would ask, *"Where would you like to go for dinner?"* I would reply, *"Wherever you would like to go would be fine with me."* This kind of exchange took place all weekend. We both tried so hard to please the other that we were totally exhausted. After returning home, we never dated each other again.

We are taught to believe that others have all the power and that they can make life good or miserable for us. This belief has never served us well. We are now discovering that ALL power is actually centered within us.

Had we both functioned from our own self-interest, we might have found some common ground. Who knows, we might even have liked each other. But instead, we had an uncomfortable weekend, and lost an opportunity to at least get to know each other better.

We can never know what is best for someone else, but if we take care of creating what is best for us, universal intelligence will handle everything else. What is truly good for any of us will turn out to be good for everyone concerned. Universal intelligence knows how to support everyone involved, even if we may not be able to see it clearly at a given time. If we can remember that we are all connected—our separateness is only in form—then we can understand how this perfect system takes care of the details if we just take care of our own business.

I do not mean to imply that we do not care about, or give consideration to, the welfare and feelings of other people. As our nervous systems become stronger, we simply begin to see and understand the perfect order in everything. Universal intelligence clearly has it all under control. When we know who we are, and that we are not separate from anyone else, our choices come from a desire to bring about the greatest good possible for everyone. We are only creating our *own* life, no one else's, and acting from our personal level of knowledge and self-interest works perfectly.

Once we begin to focus our attention inward and discover the power we have to create, it's easier to see the perfection of the system in which we live. Then we can learn to relax and go with the flow. Once we make the choice to live consciously, life takes on a totally different flavor. We learn the value of non-resistance. We stop trying to make choices for other people, and begin to simply experience whatever is present. Since we know there is a reason for whatever comes our way, we do not need to control it. When we are willing to let go of resistance and simply experience, we begin to understand the true nature of life. We can be conscious in the present moment and know that all is well.

We can never know what is best for someone else, but if we take care of creating what is best for us, universal intelligence will handle the details.

Next, let's think about creating optimal health.

Nine

Creating Optimal Health

. . .within man is the soul of the whole—
the wise silence—the universal beauty of which every
part and particle is equally related—the eternal One.

—Ralph Waldo Emerson

We want to look at our mind/body system from a somewhat different perspective than what we usually think of when we talk about creating health. Our senses tell us that our bodies are solid. Years ago, Einstein proved that everything in existence is energy. Consequently, we know that the entire mind/body system is energy and intelligence. It is, in fact, an electromagnetic energy field expressing itself in a certain form. All energy is intelligent, therefore, the energy that makes up the mind/body system has its own intelligence.

The science of quantum physics sees the world made up of vibrating particles and energy waves. Even Einstein's equation $E=MC^2$ states that there is no true distinction between energy and matter. One cubic centimeter of matter contains around a hundred million atoms. The nucleus of the atom accounts for almost all the atom's solidity, yet occupies only *one-million-millionth* of its total volume. The rest is empty space. And what is this empty space composed of? Some physicists are now calling it a *field of intelligence.*

This atomic structure is not mass, but energy. For example, the cells in the body vibrate at about a thousand times per second—molecules vibrate at a million

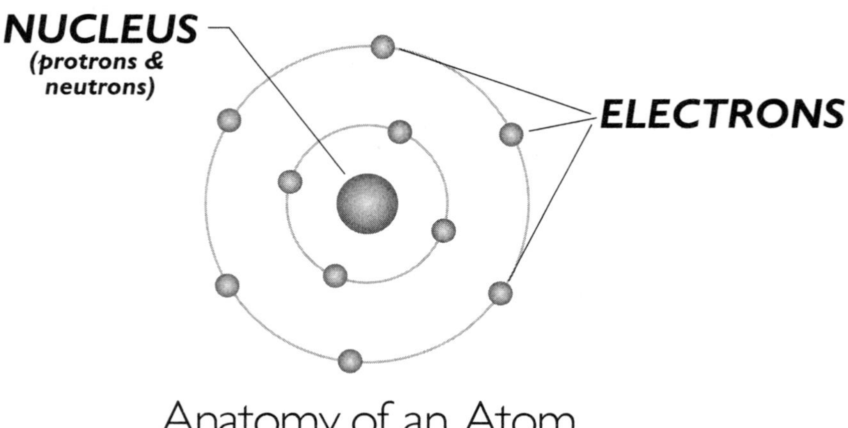

Anatomy of an Atom

times per second—atoms vibrate at a quadrillion times per second. This gives our bodies and the world around us the *appearance* of being solid.

We cannot perceive this because our five physical senses are not sensitive to the levels of light that come from the vibrating particles. If they were, we could see through the these particles and they would not appear solid to us. We have equipment to measure energy waves which we cannot see, such as gamma rays, X-rays, ultraviolet rays, infrared rays and radio waves. Our senses can detect only a fraction of the measurable energy known to us.

On the level of the Source, energy is highly refined. As the energy waves get longer they become more dense. When they get dense enough, they appear to the senses as matter. Now with the understanding that we are really not solid, but energy, let's look at how we work with this energy to create optimal health.

High-level health requires a free flow of energy, with its intelligence intact, to continually move throughout the entire mind/body system. Illness is the result of this flow of energy being blocked within the system.

High-level health requires a free flow of energy, with its intelligence intact, to continually move throughout the entire mind/body system. Illnesses are the result of this flow being blocked within the system. As we know, energy vibrates at different levels of density. Let's take a look at the different levels of energy within ourselves.

The energy that makes up the physical body is dense enough for us to see it. The conscious mind is comprised of an energy that is more refined and is *not* dense enough to be seen. The subconscious mind is even more refined than the conscious mind, and the energy of our feeling level is still more refined. Our center, our source, our inner being is the most highly refined energy possible. We can understand energy in terms of density and refinement—or faster and slower vibrations. We can also think of these vibrations as heavy or light. The slower, denser, heavier energy appears more solid.

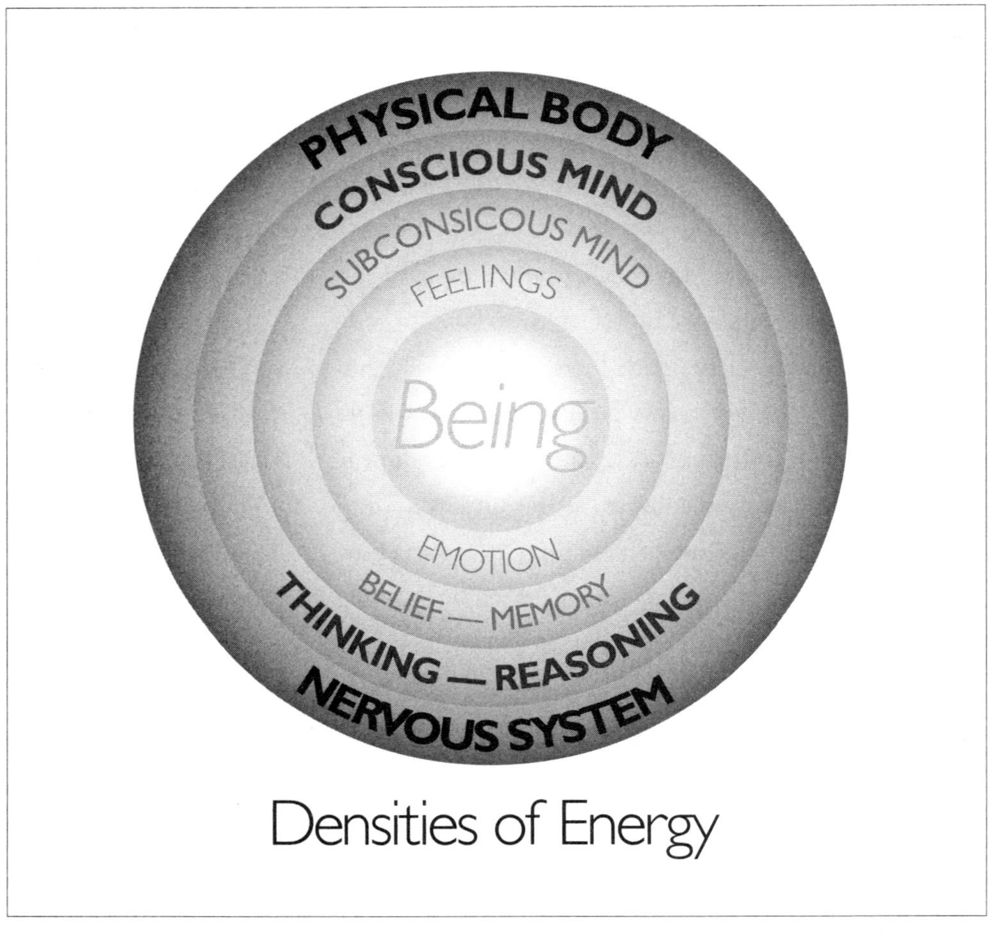

Densities of Energy

Optimal health is about the perfect connection between body, mind, emotions and spirit. In order to know who we are on the level of *Being (Spirit),* the energy of the entire body/mind system must become more refined to connect with the highly refined energy of our own inner being. In *Part Three,* I provide a process for refining the energy of the mind/body system which makes it possible for us to know ourselves on the level of the superconscious or the *Source (Being).* When the mind/body system reaches this vibratory level, we have accomplished optimal health and self-actualization. We are then capable of intuitive guidance and accessing unlimited resources to help us create the lives we want for ourselves.

Next, let's look at how our mind/body energy relates to the world around us. Since *everything in existence is energy,* and *all things are connected to one another*—every aspect of the mind/body system is affected by the energy around us.

Optimal health is all about the perfect connection between body, mind, emotions and spirit.

When we think of creating optimal health we usually think of diet and nutrition. When looking at creating health on the energy level, we know that food is also energy. There are many good books on nutrition, and also much confusion. What I want to say here is that the energy of the food we eat can only contribute the energy carried within it. Consequently, it is important to eat the freshest food possible to absorb the highest level of nutritional energy.

Another thing that is important in choosing our food is the awareness of our body's intelligence. If we are willing to experiment and to be observant, our body will tell us what it needs. It's important to trust this intelligence. Our bodies are as different and unique as our personalities. What works for one person will not necessarily work for another. *By eating according to what others say is good for us, we are actually giving away our power.*

As an example of the body's intelligence, I would like to share with you an experiment that my father-in-law tried. He owned a large chicken hatchery, and was always concerned with the best food for his chickens. He tried many different formulas because he knew they needed certain nutrients in order to produce the most eggs. One day it occurred to him that the chickens would know how to eat best for themselves if they were given a choice. In separate containers he provided all the different foods, vitamins, and minerals known to be good for chickens. Then he let them eat whatever they wanted. The results were amazing. The chickens did not all eat the same thing, but they did begin to lay far more eggs than other chickens. The method became quite popular and was known as the *free choice feeding method.* He gained a great deal of recognition for his amazing discovery.

Have you ever noticed how your body feels after eating a meal that does not contain the nutrients that it needs? For me, I feel full, but not satisfied. My body still wants something *else* to eat even though my conscious mind is finished with food for now. But still, my body knows that something is missing and tries to communicate its need. Our bodies are highly intelligent, and we would be greatly benefited by becoming aware of this intelligence.

Our bodies KNOW what foods to eat to keep us vital and healthy. We would greatly benefit from becoming aware of our body's intelligence and begin to listen to what it has to say.

In order to create optimal health, we will work with all levels of energy, the seen and the unseen.

In *Part Three,* you will be given instructions for exercising all areas of the body. These exercises work with the energy that make up the body/mind system. First, we will look at the endocrine glands. These glands secrete hormones directly into the bloodstream, and they all interact with each other. Their development and proper functioning are of great importance to our well-being. The hormones they secrete are responsible for the differences between a small person and a large person, a genius or someone of low intelligence, and the difference between a happy person and a cheerless individual. They are responsible for our energy, activity, radiance, and stability, as well as the vitalization of the life processes. Their influence is pervasive in all that we do and all that we are. They are responsible for determining the form our bodies take and the ways our minds work. Each of these glands needs to be exercised or stimulated on a regular basis in order to create optimal health.

In the same area as the endocrine glands our bodies have unseen energy centers that lie dormant until we activate them. The set of exercises in *Part Three* will allow the endocrine glands to function at their highest level. These exercises also activate the energy centers, releasing a greater supply of energy for creating health throughout the body/mind system. Practicing the routines on a daily basis will keep the entire body flexible and release stress that is stored in the nervous system. They refine our energy field and prepare the body for meditation allowing the conscious mind to merge with the superconscious. Committing to this program is one of the most powerful ways we can develop our intuitive abilities and actively discover the spiritual essence of who we truly are.

The endocrine glands secrete hormones directly into the bloodstream and are responsible for our energy, activity, radiance, and stability, as well as the vitalization of the life processes. These glands must function properly to create optimal health.

Psychological Health

The book club in the community where I live read *The End of the Affair* by Graham Greene, a perfect case study of how our energy and beliefs determine our experiences. Bendrix, the man in the affair, is very jealous. Jealousy is often a result of low self-esteem. When we feel inferior, inadequate, undesirable, or do not feel good about ourselves, we have judged ourselves according to our beliefs and that energy creates our experience. Sarah, a beautiful woman, falls in love with Bendrix. However, due to his low self-esteem, Bendrix believes that he does not deserve someone this beautiful and that she will surely leave him.

What we are all doing, at every moment, is creating lives that match our beliefs. Consequently, Bendrix sabotages the relationship right from the start. With his jealousy and fear, he creates an atmosphere that pushes his lover away. Sarah loves him very much, but they argue constantly because of his insecurity. When she finally leaves him, he is devastated, but also relieved. This brings him back into equilibrium. Sarah is gone and life again matches his beliefs without conflict.

Unfortunately, thousands of people are living their lives in this same *catch-22* situation. Our life experiences must match whatever we believe, and we will do whatever is necessary to bring this about.

The reason it is so hard for us to change our beliefs is because they are also energy and integrated into the mind/body energy field. In order to change our beliefs we must work with each part of the mind/body energy field simultaneously.

If you are in a relationship with someone who has low self-esteem there is nothing you can do to change it. No matter how great you think this person is, what he/she thinks about themselves will run their lives. In all probability you will not be able to change his/her mind.

The reason it is so hard for us to change our beliefs is because they are also energy and integrated into the mind/body energy field. In order to change our beliefs we must work with each part of the energy field simultaneously. This is why we must create a new lifestyle in order to achieve optimal health on all levels—physical, mental, emotional and spiritual.

By releasing the stress built up in the nervous system, our energy becomes refined to a level where we can merge the conscious mind with the superconscious. That is when we become aware of ourselves as whole, complete, perfect and powerful.

We begin by releasing the stress built up in the nervous system allowing the energy within the system to become more refined. Soon, the energy will be refined to a level where we are capable of bringing the conscious mind to merge with the superconscious. That is when we become aware of who we really are. We begin to know ourselves as whole, complete, perfect and powerful. Once we expand our awareness to experience ourselves on a deeper level, how could we possibly entertain thoughts that would see us as inferior, inadequate or undesirable? We come to know ourselves as Love, joy, beauty, intelligence, strength, power, whole, complete and perfect. When we reach this state of awareness, we also understand that everyone else is also part of this *wholeness.* We are never inferior or superior. We are all perfect expressions of this one Source.

Sarah, the woman in Greene's book, is married but has no intimacy with her husband. Consequently, she feels that some important part of her happiness is missing. She longs for an intimate relationship which she finds with Bendrix.

When we feel that something is missing in our lives, there is an energy that emanates from us announcing to the world that we are searching for the emptiness to be filled. This energy pours out from Sarah, and the men she meets respond to it.

We come to know ourselves as Love, joy, beauty, intelligence, strength, power, whole, complete and perfect. We are never inferior or superior. We are all perfect expressions of this one Source.

Have you ever noticed this kind of energy coming from someone? If we are observant we can feel the energy that we automatically *put out* that tells the world what is missing in our lives.

Both Bendrix and Sarah have something missing. They need spiritual understanding. They both feel incomplete and long for some sense of meaning or understanding of life. Neither believes in the traditional thinking about God. They can see the evidence that there has to be some power that governs and makes possible all the things they experience. Yet neither of them understands it. Bendrix handles his frustration by simply denying the existence of God, but Sarah could not continue to deny a higher power. Instead, she tries to find the answers to her issues by going to church. This only adds more conflicting beliefs making her life even more unbearable.

We are programmed to look to someone else for the answers to our questions. So naturally Sarah believes that she should go to a religious organization to learn about God. Whether we go to a priest, rabbi, minister or a counselor, they will tell us about their beliefs or the accepted beliefs of the organization.

Remember,

THREE — Beliefs are simply information that we have accepted as truth

This counseling may or may not be beneficial, but finding God is an inner process, not an outer one.

In *Part Three,* I lay out a process for releasing the stress that blocks our ability to go within, refine the body/mind energy, and give you techniques for meditation, which is how we connect with our source and become aware of who we are.

We are programmed to look to others for the answers to our questions. To seek our own spirituality, we need to go deep within ourselves. Only there will we connect to our source and discover the meaning in our lives.

All of us need to have meaning in our lives. We need to have some kind of experience that lets us know that there is universal order and that we are a part of it. As we work with this process for creating optimal health, we will discover our source and the *Source of all creation* right within ourselves.

In order to create the lives we want for ourselves we must start by creating optimal health. This more refined way of functioning gives us the ability to take charge of our lives and create whatever we choose.

10 Ten

Living in Harmony with the Principles of Life

Mind moves matter.

—Virgil, first century poet

Here we want to take a closer look at how life works. Our creations are governed by the seven non-changing laws of nature that we first talked about in *Chapter Five.* Through these principles, our thoughts and beliefs create our life experiences. It will be clear to see how we can create the lives we want for ourselves by living in *harmony* with these principles. The first principle we discovered is that:

ONE — *Everything in existence is Love expressing intelligently through energy*

This principle is the basis of our existence. It tells us that we are not separate entities, that we are all expressions of the One Source (Love/God)—the source of all existence. We are at one with all Love, all Intelligence and all Energy. It helps us to understand that the fulfillment of our desires is not an external process. Our desires and the fulfillment of our desires come from the same source. The only way we can keep from manifesting our desires is by over-stressing the mind/body system making it incapable of perceiving this principle and knowing our own inner self. When our nervous systems are strong and whole, we find that we can connect with all the power that exists right within ourselves. Next, let's look at our next principle, which shows us how we create our experiences. The second principle is that:

TWO — *Thought directs energy, or mind energy directs physical energy*

There is a phrase in the Bible, Philippians 4:8, which states, *"Finally, brethren, whatsoever things are true, whatsoever things are honest, whatsoever things are just, whatsoever things are pure, whatsoever things are lovely, whatsoever things are of good report—if there be any virtue, and if there be any praise, think on these things."* These were instructions on how to live successfully. Why should we focus our attention only on the good? Because whatever we focus our attention on is what we will attract into our lives.

My mother was a very religious person and she brought me to church every time the doors opened. But what I heard confused me. They said if I wanted to be saved, that I must believe. My questions were: *"Saved from what? What do I need to believe?"* The answers I got as a child didn't help me very much, but now that I understand the principle that ***thoughts or belief directs energy,*** it is clear to see that all we need to believe in is whatever we want to create. Because whatever we *actually* believe in is what we *will* create. When we come to understand this, we will be saved from much confusion and disappointment.

This principle that ***thought or beliefs direct energy*** puts us all in direct control of our own experiences. Since everything is energy, and thought directs and forms energy, this is how we create the experiences in our lives. Unfortunately, most of our beliefs have been programmed into our thinking by the people around us and the environment we live in. Most people have never taken the time to observe and explore their own beliefs—or to question them to see if they are producing the desired results. The reason for this, of course, is because most people are totally unaware of the principle, and do not realize that we are creating our own experiences through our own beliefs and thought patterns. Once we understand this principle, we can become conscious about our beliefs. When we are aware of them, we can change the ones that do not serve us well. It is my experience that this is a process over time, but the result is well worth the effort. In *Part Three,* I will give you some more guidelines for working with a step-by-step process that will make it possible for you to take charge of your life and work in harmony with this principle.

Two of the other principles that are important to consider here are that:

THREE — *Beliefs are simply information that we have accepted as truth*

and that:

FOUR — *Everything in the relative world is always changing*

These principles *guarantee* that we are in charge of our own lives. What makes a belief true for us is our own perception. Truth is whatever we choose to believe in. I am sure we have all heard two people, who had the same experience, describe it in totally opposite ways. For example, the experience of losing a job. Several people may lose their jobs at the same time. One person will be totally devastated, filled with fear and uncertainty, while another will feel exhilarated and excited about the prospects for the future. How we react to any situation is determined by our own thoughts and beliefs—by the things we say to ourselves. If we believe ***all things work together for good,*** then we will look for the good in all situations we encounter. And guess what? We usually find it. If we believe we are losers and nothing ever works out right for us, we'll find that, too. The exciting thing is that by choosing new beliefs our experiences will change accordingly. By living in harmony with these principles we will create whatever we want. The next principle we want to look at is:

FIVE — *The law of attraction and repulsion— what comes from us returns to us*

This law assures us that whatever we can create in our minds, we can create in our experiences. It works in a very automatic way, as all laws of nature do. Every single thought we think is affected by this principle. Thoughts are mental energy, and they attract to themselves the complementary physical and emotional energy necessary to fulfill our visions and expectations. Consequently, we want to keep our thoughts focused on the kind of things we want to experience.

By now you are probably saying, "*Wait a minute. I have experienced many things that I had never thought about or expected would ever happen to me.*" First, let's remember that most of our beliefs are not on the conscious level. But in addition, certain things will simply come up in our lives for our growth. Eastern philosophy relates most of these things to what is called karma, or the opportunity to balance out the actions made in a previous life. Whether you believe in karma or previous lifetimes is irrelevant. It suffices to say that we will each face certain challenges, or what appear to be unfortunate situations, in our life. We may have never thought of the occurrence, but we do have choices about how we deal with it. This brings us to the next principle we want to consider:

SIX — *We all make our own choices*

NOW is the only time in existence. Whatever is in the *NOW* is what we must deal with. It doesn't change anything to whine, complain or wish things were different. The only way we can grow or change anything is to make choices about *what IS*. If we don't like what is happening in our lives, for the most part we can change it. But, it is a process over time. Some things are not changeable, like the death of someone close to you. We cannot change the occurrence, but we can choose how we react to it. Whatever the situation, we always have choices, and our choices will always relate to our beliefs. If we know we have choices and can make things different—make things better—we can deal with whatever *IS* in a constructive way. This principle, again, gives us the *power* to create the lives we want for ourselves.

The last principle we want to look at is that:

SEVEN — *Giving and receiving are two sides of the same coin*

These seven principles give us *everything* we need to create *whatever* we want. However, in order for *anything* to happen, the circle must be completed. We must be willing and capable of receiving our desires. Again, *we* get to choose. We do not have to receive anything that we do not want, nor do we have to give anything we do not want to give. When we learn how to ***fully accept only good in our lives, it is only good that we have to give,*** and everyone gets to choose what they will accept.

It is easy to see that we can create magnificent lives for ourselves. By connecting to the Love, directing our thought energy through chosen beliefs, we attract the experiences that will change our lives. We can *"have it all"* if we choose to do so and open to receive the gifts of our own creation.

In summary, here are the seven laws of nature, or principles of life, that are governing how we create our experiences:

1. *Everything in existence is Love expressing intelligently through energy*
2. *Thought (belief) directs energy*
3. *Beliefs are simply information that we have accepted as truth*
4. *Everything in the relative world is always changing*
5. *The law of attraction and repulsion—what comes from us returns to us*
6. *We all make our own choices*
7. *Giving and receiving are two sides of the same coin*

In the next section we will present a life-changing process that will make it possible to live your life on a totally new level and launch you onto a path to create your OWN unlimited futures!

PART THREE

From Caterpillars to Butterflies

11

Eleven

A New Lifestyle — A New Life

Truth is not introduced into the individual from without, but within him all the time.

—Sören Kierkegaard, nineteenth century Danish philosopher

It is now time to begin spinning our cocoons, creating a place that makes it possible for us to experience our own metamorphosis. It is now time to create a lifestyle that will allow us to experience self-actualization.

The first step is commitment. Consider W. H. Murray's statement: *"Until one is committed there is hesitancy, the chance to draw back, always ineffectiveness. Concerning all acts of initiative (and creation), there is one elementary truth, the ignorance of which kills countless ideas and splendid plans: the moment one definitely commits oneself, then providence moves, too. All sorts of things occur to help that would never otherwise have occurred. A whole stream of events issues from the decisions, raising in one's favor all manner of unforeseen incidents, meetings and material assistance, which no man could have dreamt would have come his way."*

All accomplishments require commitment. I hope by now you are ready to make a full commitment to creating a lifestyle that will lead you to higher and higher levels of personal growth and self-actualization. Creating this new lifestyle is the most important thing you have to do if you want to create this new way of functioning for yourself.

There is a routine of things that you need to do on a daily basis in order to refine the energy in the mind/body system so that it is capable of merging with the more refined energy of the superconscious.

We know that everything is made up of energy, and energy vibrates from low levels of density—a rock, for example—to higher levels of refinement which we find in human beings. However, the ordinary person's energy is not sufficiently refined to allow him to intuitively know himself.

The stress in our lives blocks our ability to know who we are on a higher level. In order to release the stress stored in the mind/body system and refine the energy which makes up the system, we must make a commitment to a daily routine of breathing exercises, stretching exercises and meditation. When we schedule these practices into our daily lives, our lives begin to change—however, you may or may not feel the subtle changes in the energy in your mind and body. Either way, the energy will begin to change and you will feel peaceful and calm inside. The mind will stop racing constantly and thoughts will become clearer. Your ability to focus your attention will improve.

These are subtle changes that have accumulative effects over time. Please do not expect fireworks—this is an inner process, not an outer one.

It is also highly recommended that you eliminate as much stress as possible from your life. Many things cause stress, the major one being our own thoughts and beliefs. We will work with our beliefs later. For now, start to observe how you feel when you are in the company of different people. Try to associate with people who bring a positive energy and with whom you feel good. You will discover that you feel uplifted after being in the presence of some people, and drained of your energy after being with others. Also, notice how you are affected by entertainment. Some entertainment will leave you feeling uplifted, while some others will leave you drained.

When we schedule these practices into our daily lives, we begin to change. These are subtle changes that accumulate over time helping to make it possible to create the lives we've always dreamed of.

One of the most powerful tools we have to use for our growth is observation. As we observe how we relate to the energy around us, our consciousness expands and we are able to make better choices. Remember that you are in charge— you get to make all of your own choices *and* experience all the consequences.

Let's get started with the breathing and stretching exercises that will start to refine the mind/body energy. First, choose a place where you can be alone and not be disturbed while doing your routine. It is beneficial to have a special blanket that you use just for these exercises.

It is recommended that you start your day with this process, and repeat it in the early evening if you want to grow as fast as possible. In the morning, practice it before breakfast—in the evening, before dinner—always on an empty stomach. If you choose to do the exercises in the late evening, wait at least three hours after eating.

We have named these stretching exercises—*Energizers*—to help you understand that they have a totally different purpose than aerobics, running, or calisthenics. These energizers activate the energy centers in the body that lie dormant if not activated. This activation not only gives more energy, it also allows the stress stored in the body to be released. It allows the body to become settled, thereby allowing the mind to calm itself. This brings the entire system to a state of deep rest. It is the nature of the system, given sufficient rest, to heal and strengthen itself. Each of the energizers has a physically healing effect and will strengthen specific areas of the body. Performing *all* of the energizers in the *following order* provides revitalization for the entire physiology.

The breath is the link between the mind and body. Proper breathing is an important part of becoming peaceful.

Deep breathing—bringing the air all the way down to the abdomen—is a reliable way to keep the mind sharp and help alleviate stress.

These are relaxing exercises and need to be performed slowly and smoothly. Never force or strain. You want to allow your body to relax into the posture. This process is for *both* the mind and body. Consequently, we need to keep our mind focused on the body while doing the exercises. You want to be totally *with* the body, to experience how it feels as it moves. Bring your attention to whatever area of the body you are working with, and become fully aware of that area of your body. This begins to expand our awareness of the inter-relatedness of the mind and body, and develops the mind's ability to focus.

We start the process in the morning with three purifying breaths. Go outside, or at least get your head outside, and take a deep breath, inhaling through the nose. Then, exhale forcefully through the mouth, releasing all the stale air that has settled in the lungs overnight. Do this three times, no more. It is helpful to use the arms and hands as though you are pulling the air in and throwing it out.

Now, come inside, spread your blanket and let's get started. Sit in the middle of the blanket in a comfortable cross-legged position. We want to start with a breathing exercise. First, you want to notice your usual way of breathing, and observe how deep breaths and shallow breaths affect your energy. Place your hand on your abdomen, and inhale deeply, as though you are bringing the air all the way down into the abdomen. Your abdomen should expand as you breathe in. Now, exhale, releasing all the air, pulling in the abdomen. Notice how you feel as you continue to take these deep breaths. ***This is the way we should always breathe.*** This gives

This type of breathing on a regular basis will begin to bring the mind and body into synchronicity building a much stronger mind/body connection.

1 one

PURIFYING BREATHS

- *Go outside*
- *Inhale through the nose, out through the mouth*
- *Arms at your side, swing them up (bending at the elbows) towards your chest on the inhale*
- *Arc them back down to your sides on the exhale*
- *Repeat three cycles*

Purifying breaths release the stale air in your lungs and replace it with fresh oxygen, ready to activate your nervous system

you maximum use of the oxygen in the air, and also creates a relaxed, peaceful feeling. Just for comparison, let's also try a shallow breath. Place your hand on the upper part of your chest. Now, breathe into the chest only. Notice how the shallow breath makes you feel. The breath automatically becomes shallow when we feel anxious.

Notice your breathing periodically throughout the day. If you find your breath is shallow and short, consciously change it to the long deep breaths as described above. The breath is the link between the mind and body, and this form of breathing on a regular basis will begin to bring the mind and body into synchronicity.

2 two

BEGINNING BREATHING

- *Sit in a comfortable cross-legged position*
- *Notice your "normal" way of breathing*
- *Place your hands on your abdomen*
- *Inhale deeply, bringing air all the way down to your stomach*
- *Let your abdomen fully expand as your bring the air all the way down*
- *Exhale, releasing all the air pulling in the abdomen*
- *THIS IS THE WAY WE SHOULD ALWAYS BREATHE*

Deep, slow breathing—starting in the chest bringing the breaths all the way down to the abdomen—releases tension and calms the mind

Now, we begin the stretching exercises we call the ***Energizers.*** To prepare the body, we start with *#3, Self-Massage.* Begin by pressing gently on your forehead with the palms of your hands. Move over your eyes, down the face and neck to your heart. Now, clasp your hands together and apply pressure to the back of your head. Move the hands apart, massage over the shoulders and back to the heart.

Now, hold one arm out as if you are going to shake hands with someone. Then take the other hand and start massaging the hand and arm, up the top side of the arm, and down to the heart. Massage the hand and arm up the bottom side and down to the heart. Do the same thing with the other hand and arm. Next, take one foot into both of your hands and massage the foot and up the leg with one hand on

each side of the leg, then bring one hand up the front of the body and one up the back to the heart. Repeat with the other leg.

Next, we go to ***#4, the Body Roll.*** Lie flat on your back, bend your knees and, bringing them to your chest, clasp your hands together over your legs. Now, roll to your right, keeping your head on the floor. Bring your head all the way around so

four 4

The BODY ROLL
- *Keep head on the floor*
- *Roll to the forehead*
- *Bring head around so to look in the other direction*

that you are looking back the other way. Now, roll to the left the same way. Perform this exercise ten times, five each way.

After the rolls, go into ***#5, the Bicycle,*** moving your legs as you would pedal a bicycle. Continue for about ten to twenty times and then stretch the body out. After a good stretch, bring your arms down to your side, palms up, and totally relax. Remain in this relaxed position for about three minutes.

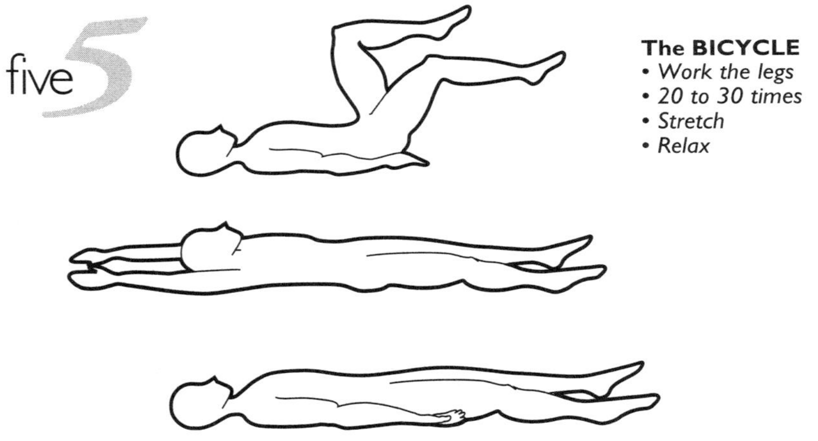

Now we move to ***#6, the Toner*** *(see next page).* Stand on your knees with your hands clasped together, palms up, in front of you. Push your arms and hands down while tightening the buttocks and leaning your shoulders backward. Hold this position for a count of ten.

Next we go to ***#7, the Back Arch*** *(see next page).* Place your hands on the floor behind you as you sit back on your heels, then lift your body up off the legs. Be gentle. If you notice that you are straining your body—pause for a couple of moments. Remember that this is NOT about being an expert at the movements.

THE TONER
- *In a kneeling position*
- *Hands clasped in front*
- *Push down with your hands*
- *Tighten the buttocks*
- *Lean backward*
- *Hold for ten seconds*

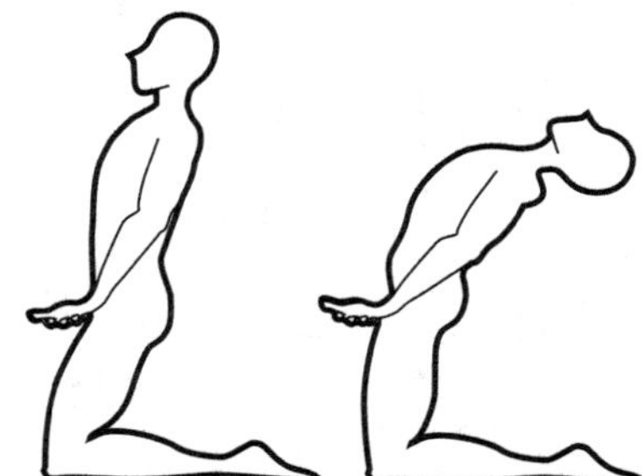

Mastery will come in time. It IS about balancing the mind and body by releasing stress. Any form of pain or strain is evidence that you are creating MORE stress. It is counter-productive. Perform each exercise only to the degree that it is slightly stretching for you. As you continue to do the exercises daily you will become more limber, and it will get easier and easier. You are getting EXACTLY what you need if you are stretching, but not hurting yourself. If for any reason you should hurt yourself, even slightly, discontinue the exercise until your body has healed itself.

THE BACK ARCH
- *Start from a kneeling position*
- *Place your hands on the floor behind you as you sit back on your heals*
- *Gently lift your body off your legs*
- *Slightly arching your back*
- *Let your head fall backward*
- *Eventually hold for twenty seconds*

THE CAMEL

- *Standing on your knees*
- *Lean back*
- *Grab your ankles for support*
- *Let your head fall gently back*
- *Evenutually hold for twenty seconds*

Now to ***#8, the Camel.*** Bring the body up straight on your knees, then bring your shoulders down bending at your lower back. Place your hands on your ankles to support you. Remember, you do not have to do it perfectly at first. Let your body get used to these postures at its own pace. Simply leaning back is a good place to start.

Next is ***#9, Limbering the Legs and the Lotus Position.*** Start this posture in a comfortable sitting position. Place one leg out in front of you. Take the other leg by the ankle and bring the free arm around the knee, as if you are holding a

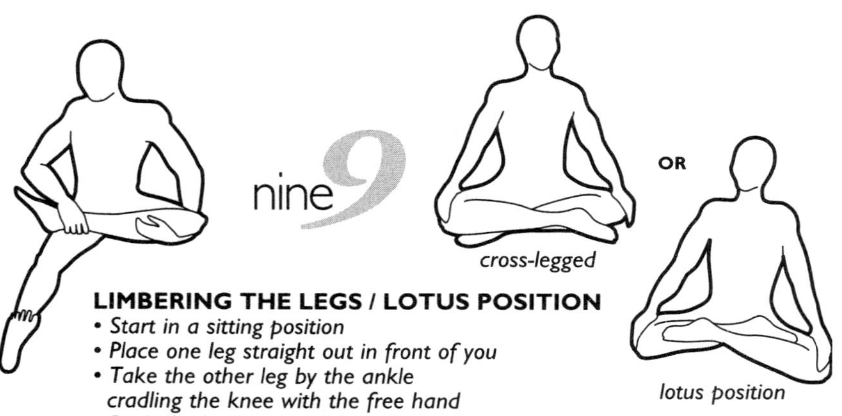

LIMBERING THE LEGS / LOTUS POSITION

- *Start in a sitting position*
- *Place one leg straight out in front of you*
- *Take the other leg by the ankle cradling the knee with the free hand*
- *Rock the leg back and forth, limbering it up*
- *Repeat on the other side*

baby. Then, rock the leg back and forth, just limbering it up, about five times. Repeat the same procedure with the other leg. Then, move into a cross-legged or lotus position.

After a number of months of practice, your legs and hips may be limber enough for the *Lotus Position.* Begin by placing one foot on the top of the opposite thigh, then bring the other leg over the top of the first leg and tuck the foot behind the knee. Do not try to force this in any way. It took me three years to be able to sit in this position yet my husband could do it right away. Our natural ability to hold these postures is determined by how we are built. Please be observant and respectful of your body. Once you master this position, it becomes very comfortable and will hold your back straight for other postures. Until you are comfortable with the lotus position, just sit in a comfortable cross-legged position.

THE NECK ROLL

- *Let your chin drop to your chest*
- *Slowly roll your head around in one direction*
- *Three full rotations in each direction*

#10, the Neck Roll. This keeps the neck limber and releases the stress stored there. Let your chin fall toward your chest, and slowly roll your head all the way around. Do this three times in each direction.

After the neck roll, move to *#11, Drop Ear to Shoulder.* Face straight ahead, then bring your right ear down toward your right shoulder. Hold for a couple of seconds, then repeat on the left side. Repeat twice.

DROP EAR TO SHOULDER

- *Look straight ahead*
- *Bring your right ear down to your right shoulder, hold–2–3*
- *Bring your head up straight*
- *Bring your left ear down to your left shoulder, hold–2–3*
- *Repeat twice*

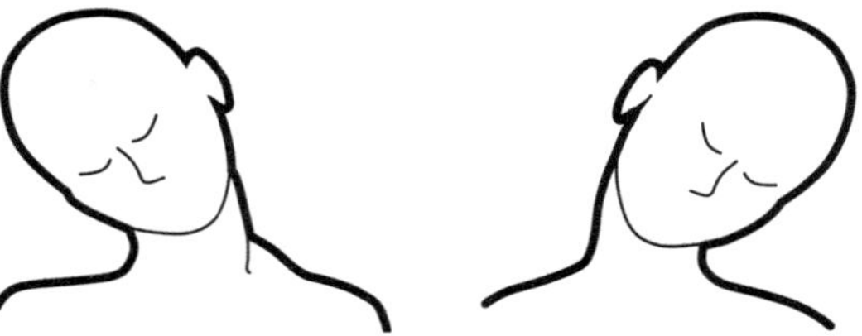

#12, Chin-Eye exercise, is performed by jutting the chin out and turning the head as far as possible to the right, and at the same time stretching the eyes to the right looking behind you as far as you can. This is a great eye exercise for peripheral vision and it also allows light to stimulate the pituitary gland. Repeat the movement two times on each side.

CHIN–EYE EXERCISE

- *Jutt out your chin*
- *Eyes WIDE open*
- *Turn your head as far to the right as you can*
- *Stretch your eyes looking behind you*
- *Repeat on the left side*
- *Two times on each side*

Now to ***#13, the Forward Bend.*** At first this will be done from a cross-legged position, but after you are comfortable, use the lotus position instead. Bring your arms out straight in front of you palms touching. Turn the hands over so the backs of the hands are now touching, palms facing outward. Arc your arms behind your back and clasp your hands together. Pull the arms up as high as you can while bending forward toward the floor in front of you. Hold this position for about ten seconds. Gently release your hands and return to a normal sitting position.

- *Sit in a cross-legged or lotus position*
- *(1) Bring your arms out straight in front of you, palms facing inward*
- *(2) Turn your hands placing them back to back, palms facing outward*
- *Arc your arms around your body and, (3) clasp your hands behind you*
- *(4) Pull your arms up as high as you can, bending at the waist, bringing your head toward the floor*
- *Hold this for ten seconds*

Next, we move to ***#14, the Backward Bend.*** Still in this cross-legged position, or lotus, bring your hands behind you placing your fingertips on the floor at the base of your hips. Your hands should be facing forward, palms flat to the floor. Gently lean back resting your weight on your elbows and lower arms. Slowly, let your head fall backward. Hold this position for about ten seconds. This should be a very comfortable stretch. Remember, your movements should be soft and easy. If you strain yourself by *forcing* a posture, you are not doing yourself any good. Releasing stress is our intent. Pushing yourself beyond your current limits of flexibility only serves to bring more stress into the body rather than releasing it.

fourteen 14

THE BACKWARD BEND

- *Start in cross-legged or lotus position*
- *Bring your hands behind you fingers facing forward*
- *Gently lean back resting your weight on your forearms*
- *Let your head fall backward*
- *Slightly arching your back*
- *Hold for ten seconds*

Next, we have ***#15, Arm Circles*** *(see next page).* Sit in a comfortable cross-legged position, holding your arms out straight to your sides. Make as large a circle as possible moving both arms at the same time. Bring your arms up as high as you can, and just skim the floor on the downward arc. Circle your arms in a forward motion for ten times, then reverse and circle in the opposite direction.

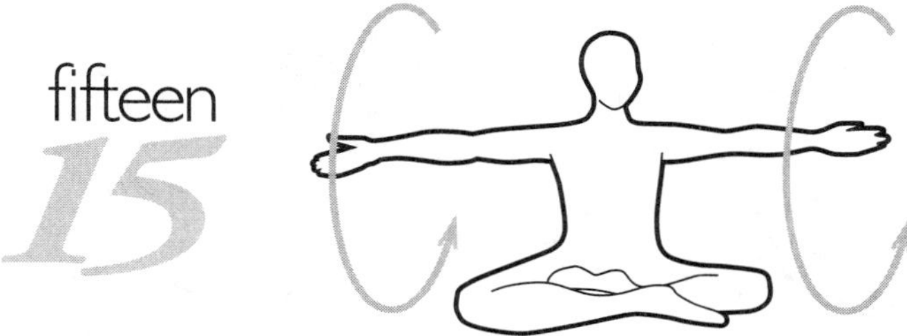

ARM CIRCLES

- *Sit in a comfortable cross-legged or lotus position*
- *Hold your arms out straight on each side*
- *Make as large a circle as possible, bringing your arms up as high as you can, then down, just skimming the floor. First a forward motion ten times, then reverse for ten times*

Now, on to ***#16, Upper Arm Tension.*** There are two movements in this energizer. First, bring your hands together in front of you, palms facing together, elbows up. Push the palms together until you feel the muscles in the upper arms and chest tighten. Now, move your arms side-to-side, pivoting at the shoulders. Repeat six times. For the second movement, point your hands upward. Rotate your hands forward and back. Repeat six times.

UPPER ARM TENSION

- *Sit in a comfortable cross-legged or lotus position*
- *Press hands together, palms facing, elbows up*
- *Push palms together feeling the muscles in the upper arms and chest tighten*
- *There are two movements. (1) Move your arms side-to-side, pivoting at the shoulders*
- *(2) With hands still pressed together, rotate both hands front-and-back, pivoting at the wrists*

STRETCH OVER KNEE

- *Start in a sitting position — put one leg out in front of you*
- *Bend the other knee and place the sole of the foot as close to the crotch as possible*
- *Hold the outstretched leg with your hands, gently lean your body forward, head to knee*
- *Hold to a count of twenty and then repeat with the other leg*

Let's move to ***#17, Stretch Over Knee.*** In a sitting position, bring one leg straight out in front of you. Bend the other knee and place the sole of the foot against the inside of your leg as close to the crotch as possible. Now, hold the outstretched leg with your hands and lean your body forward, bringing the head toward the knee. Be gentle. If you can only bow your head to begin with, that is a perfect start. Hold this position and start with a count of ten and build up to a count of twenty. Repeat the posture with the other leg.

Next we go to ***#18, Plow with Shoulder Stand*** *(see next page)*. If you have a back problem of any kind, please check with your physician before doing this exercise. Start from a sitting position, with legs straight out in front of your body. Grasp the legs with each hand at any place that works for you, then bring your head down toward your knees. Release the legs, bend your knees and roll up and backward, bringing your legs over your head. Place your arms on the floor and support your back with both hands on your waist. Now, tuck your chin into the hollow space just below your neck and bring your legs up as straight as possible. Hold this position for a count of ten, building to twenty. Come down by bending your knees and rolling out smoothly. Move gently back into a sitting position, then repeat the exercise one more time.

eighteen 18

PLOW

- *Start from a sitting position, legs straight out in front*
- *(1) Grasp your legs with each hand and bring your head toward your knees*
- *(2) Release the legs, bend your knees, (3) roll up and backwards*

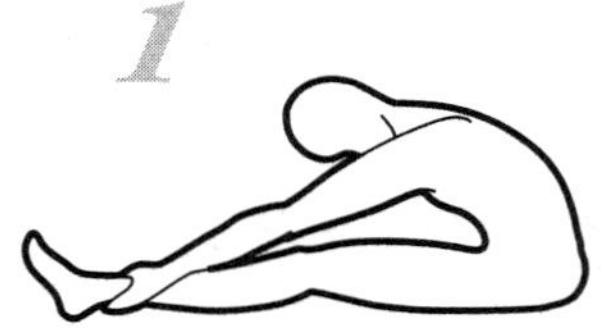

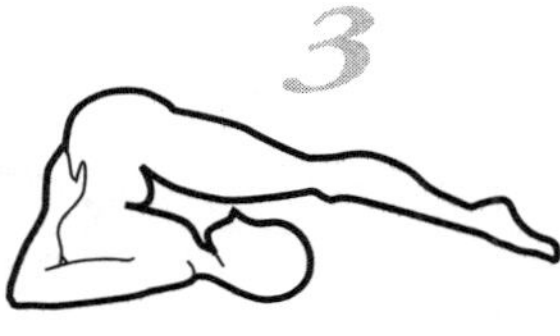

WITH SHOULDER STAND

- *(4) Tuck your chin into the hollow part of your neck*
- *(5) Bring your legs up as straight as possible, holding for a count of twenty*
- *(6) Come down by bending your knees and, (7) rolling out smoothly*
- *(8) Move gently back into a sitting position, then repeat entire exercise one more time*

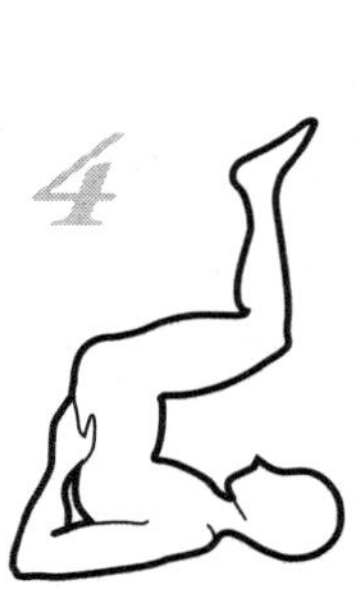

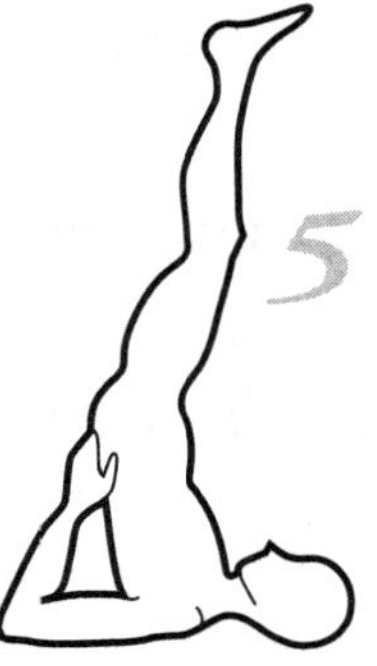

This brings us to ***#19, Feet Together—Knees to Floor.*** Bring the soles of your feet together. Hold them with your hands and bring your knees downward towards the floor, giving your thighs a good stretch.

FEET TOGETHER — KNEES TO FLOOR
- *Bring the soles of your feet together*
- *Hold your feet with your hands, keeping your feet in contact*
- *Bring your knees down to the floor*

Next is ***#20, Straddle Leg Splits.*** Stretch your legs in front of you as far as is comfortable. Place one hand on each leg and bring your head toward the floor between your legs. Again, be easy with yourself. I have seen people who could only bow their heads and others who were very limber and easily could put their heads to the floor. Again, you only want to do what is a comfortable stretch for you.

STRADDLE LEG SPLITS
- *Angle your legs out in front of you*
- *Stretch apart as far as is comfortable*
- *Grasp each leg as close to the ankle as possible*
- *Bring your head down as close to the floor as you can*

#21, Total Relaxation is just what we need now. The next few exercises will be done from a horizontal position on the floor, and you should rest between each of them. How long you rest depends on how much time you have allotted, but please do not skip the rests. The rest periods are just as important as the exercises. The idea is to stretch the body, then totally relax it.

For this version of ***Total Relaxation,*** lie flat on the floor, on your stomach. Arms should be down by your sides, palms up. Do not place arms over the head. When relaxing, always have arms down by your side. This is also an exercise for the neck. Lie the face flat on the floor on one side, then alternate to the other side—looking to the left after one exercise and the right after the next. This first relaxation should last at least three minutes. You can count or determine the time by feel.

twentyone

21

TOTAL RELAXATION

- *Lay down on your stomach, arms at your sides*
- *Pay attention to your breathing. Breathe deeply. Release all tension. Relax the mind.*

Pay attention to your breathing. You can also place your attention on various parts of the body or just feel yourself melt into the floor or carpeting. Let your thoughts drift away. Your breathing will start to slow and you will feel a deep sense of relaxation and well-being spread throughout your body. Enjoy this sensation as you become more and more peaceful.

22 twentytwo

THE COBRA

- *Bring your head straight up from the floor*
- *Bend your elbows, hands facing each other*
- *Push up, lifting your head and shoulders higher*
- *Turn your neck to one side looking at the opposite foot*
- *Return to center and look to the other side*
- *Rest and repeat once more*

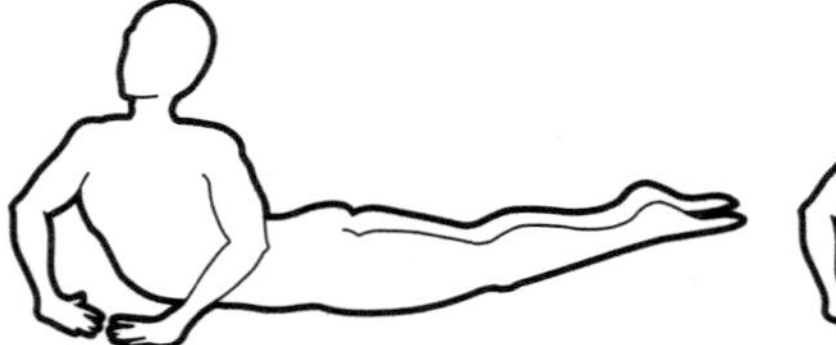

Now, you are ready for *#22, the Cobra.* Lift your head and neck straight up off the floor. Place your hands flat on the floor in front of you, facing each other. Bend your elbows and push backward, lifting your chest off the floor, but keep your stomach touching the floor. Keeping the elbows bent, turn your neck and eyes to where you can see the heel of the opposite foot on one side—then turn your head in the other direction and check the other foot. When you first start the exercises you might need to raise your foot off the floor a little to help get it in your range of sight. Now, rest and then repeat the cobra exercise once more.

twentythree 23

THE BODY ROCK

- *Start by lying on your stomach*
- *Bend one knee and grasp the ankle with your hand*
- *Take the other foot with your free hand*
- *Make your body into a "rocker"*
- *Lift head, chest and knees off the floor*
- *"Rock" back and forth five times building up to ten*

Next, we move to ***#23, the Body Rock*** *(see previous page)*. From the resting position, bend one knee and bring the leg up to where you can grasp the ankle with your hand. Now, do the same with your other leg making a rocker of your body. Get a firm grip of your ankles, then lift the head and chest off the floor. Once you are in this position, hold it for a count of ten, then begin to rock. Rock back and forth five times, building up to ten over time. Now, relax again. This may be a bit of a challenge at first—do whatever feels right and works for you.

Again, it is important to note that these energizers are about releasing stress from the mind/body system, NOT about performing a posture with *perfect* precision. Listen to what your body tells you. If a movement feels too strenuous, try a version of the posture that is more basic. If you strain or feel pain, this is your body telling you to STOP. Listen to it. Never use force—this only slows your progress. As you continue to work with the energizers, your body will limber up. Keep practicing the postures, making adjustments as you go, and one day it will go into the position easily.

Once the body feels totally relaxed again, move on to ***#24, the Leg Lift.*** Still lying on your stomach, bring your arms down by your side. Make two fists with your hands and tighten each arm all the way up to the shoulders. Press down on your fists and arms while lifting your legs up from the floor without bending your knees. Hold this position for a count of ten, building to twenty. Rest, then repeat.

24
twentyfour

THE LEG LIFT

- *Lying on your stomach, make both hands into fists*
- *Lock your elbows and press down into the floor*
- *Raise your legs without bending your knees*
- *Hold for a count of ten, building to twenty*
- *Rest and then repeat once more*

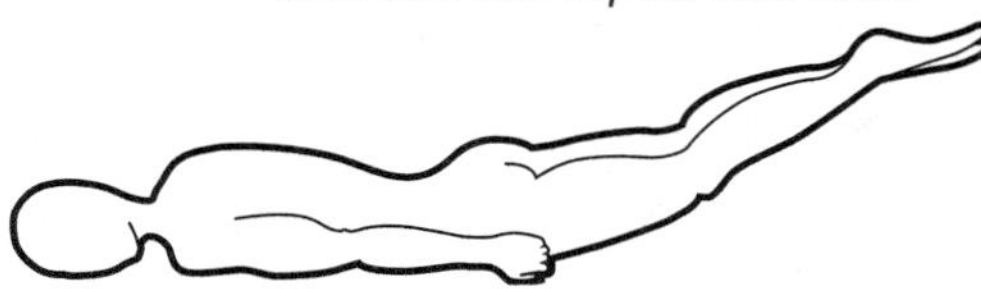

From your rest position move on to ***#25, the Cat Stretch.*** Bring your hands up in front of you, then push your body up, arching the back. Now, keeping your hands flat on the floor, stretch backward to where you are sitting on your lower legs and ankles with the head and body stretched out in front of you. Hold this position for a count of ten, building to twenty. This posture is done two different times, before and after *the Balance* position. It is a very relaxing posture that gives the entire body a good stretch.

THE CAT STRETCH
- *Bring your hands down in front of you*
- *Push your body up, stretching your back*
- *Keep your hands flat on the floor and stretch backwards*
- *Sit on your lower legs and ankles with your head and body stretched out in front of you*

From this position go directly into ***#26, the Balance*** *(see next page).* Balance your weight on your right knee and your left hand, then bring your left leg and your right arm up to a balanced position. Keep your sight on the right hand that is up out in front of you. Hold this position for a count of ten, building to twenty. Now, repeat on the other side. Balance your weight on the left knee and the right hand, bringing the right leg and the left arm up, keeping your eyes on the left hand. Now, rest again.

26 twentysix

THE BALANCE

- *Start from a kneeling position—lift your left leg and right hand*
- *Balance your weight on your LEFT hand and RIGHT leg*
- *Stretch out you left leg and right hand looking at the right hand*
- *Hold for a count of ten, building to twenty*
- *Repeat on the other side*

Now, move on to *#27,* which is just a repeat of the cat stretch one more time. After this, move into a sitting position.

27 twentyseven

THE CAT STRETCH

- *Bring your hands down in front of you*
- *Push your body up, stretching your back*
- *Keep your hands flat on the floor and stretch backwards*
- *Sit on your lower legs and ankles with your head and body stretched out in front of you*

This brings us to *#28, the Twist.* From a sitting position, bring the *left* leg straight out in front of you. Now, bend the knee of the *right* leg and place the *right* foot flat on the floor on the left side of the left knee. Put your *right* arm behind you. Bring your *left* arm behind the far side of the *right* knee and hold onto the *right* ankle. Now, twist your body to the right looking as far behind you as possible. Hold for a count of five, then turn the head to look over your left shoulder, and hold for a count of five. Repeat the entire procedure on the other side, with your *right* leg out straight, bring your *left* foot on the outer side of the *right* knee. Put the *left* hand behind you and bring your *right* arm around the outside of your *left* leg and twist your body and head to look over your *right* shoulder. This will take some concentration for beginners, but you will experience a very nice stretch. Repeat two times on each side.

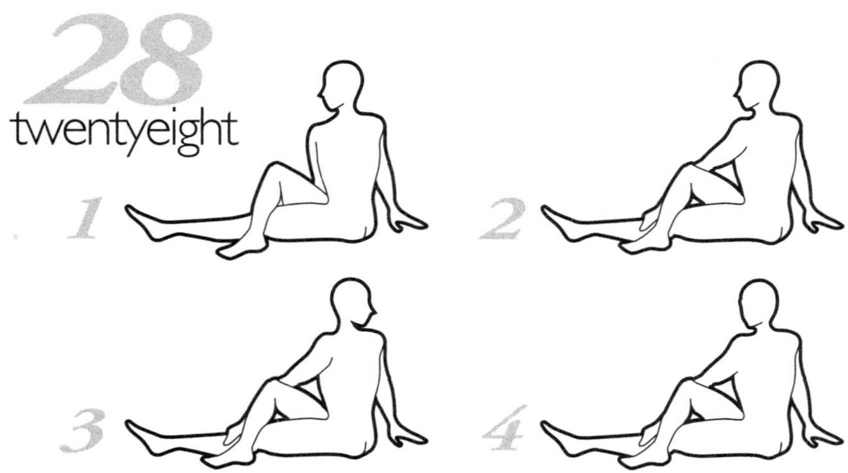

THE TWIST

- *Seated—with your LEFT leg straight out in front of you, bend your RIGHT leg at the knee*
- *(1) Place your RIGHT foot flat on the floor on the opposite side of the LEFT leg*
- *(2) Place your RIGHT arm behind you and reach your LEFT arm behind the other side of the RIGHT knee and hold onto the RIGHT ankle*
- *(3) Twist your body to the right looking as far behind you as possible*
- *(4) Hold for a count of five, then turn the head to look over your left shoulder*
- *Now, repeat the entire progression with your RIGHT leg out straight, bending your LEFT leg*

Next, we move to ***#29, the Tummy Pops.*** If you are not a belly dancer, we are going to focus on some muscles that you probably haven't used for a while. We start from a cross-legged sitting position. Take a deep, full breath and bring the air all the way down into the stomach. Remember, this is how we want to be breathing all the time now. Then exhale. After exhaling, and before inhaling again, pull the stomach muscles in and up, and *pop* them in and out a few times before inhaling again. Be easy with this movement. At the beginning, just go with the timing that feels right for your breathing. First, do one or two. Then do ten, building up to twenty. The second position is where you are kneeling on your hands and knees. Repeat the full breath, and after exhaling, pull your stomach in and up—*pop* it in and out. Finally, move to a standing position. Place your feet apart, about shoulder width. Bend your knees and place your hands on your knees, fingers facing inward. Repeat the full breath, and after you exhale bring your stomach in and up, then *pop* it in and out several times before inhaling again.

THE TUMMY POPS

- *(1) Start in a seated, cross-legged position – take a full, deep breath expanding the stomach*
- *Exhale ALL the air, pull stomach muscles in & up, and POP them a few times before inhaling*
- *(2) Move into a kneeling position – take in a deep breath and POP the stomach in and out*
- *(3) Standing, bend slightly at the knees, hands on thighs – breathe deep and POP the stomach*
- *At first, do one or two – then ten – eventually working up to 20 POPs at a time*

This brings us to ***#30, Upper Body Twist and Bend.*** Stand straight with arms reaching as high as possible above your head. Turn your body at the waist as far to the right as you can, then back to the left. Repeat two times on each side. End the movement by looking straight ahead and bend your body at the waist to bring your hands and arms down toward the floor. Whatever level you can reach is fine. In time, you will most likely be able to put your hands flat on the floor.

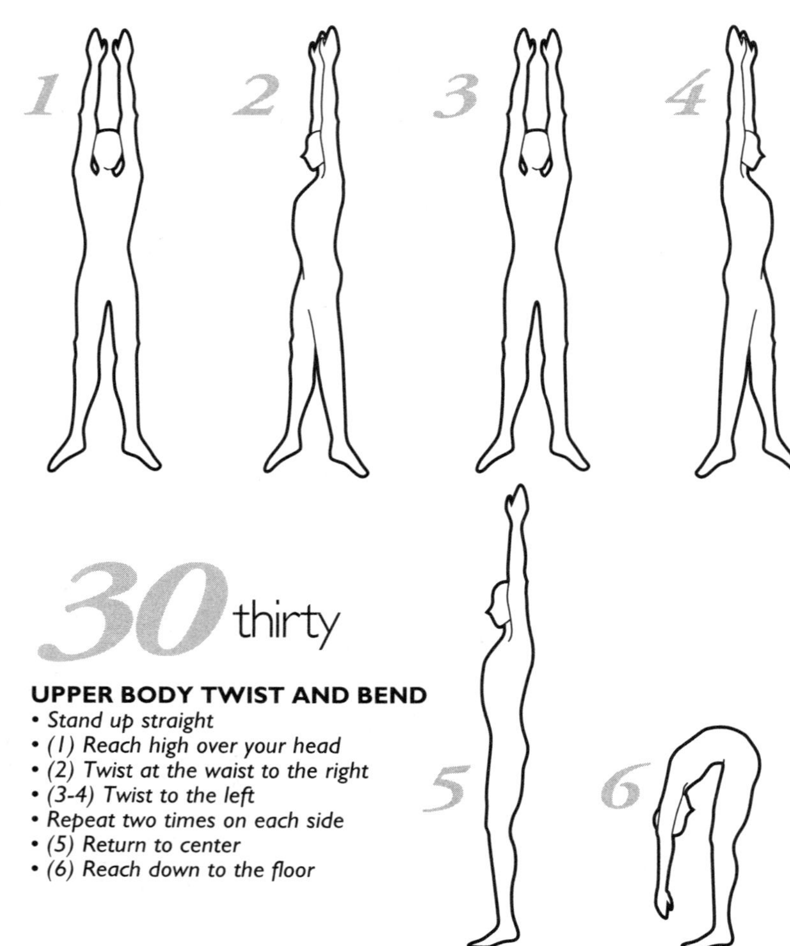

UPPER BODY TWIST AND BEND

- *Stand up straight*
- *(1) Reach high over your head*
- *(2) Twist at the waist to the right*
- *(3-4) Twist to the left*
- *Repeat two times on each side*
- *(5) Return to center*
- *(6) Reach down to the floor*

This brings us to *#31, Bounce and Shake.* Come back to a standing position and shake out the arms and legs. Then, bounce up and down about 20 times. You can run in place or back and forth on your blanket for whatever feels right, building to a count of 100. Now, shake your body like a dog shaking the water off his body, then lie down on your back and rest.

31 thirtyone

BOUNCE AND SHAKE

- *Shake out the arms and legs*
- *Bounce up and down 20 times*
- *Run in place counting up to 100 or*
- *Run around the blanket*
- *Shake your body like a dog shaking water of its body*
- *Lie down on your back and relax*

This brings us to *#32, Total Relaxation.* This time we relax on the back. Lie down flat on your back, arms down by your sides with your palms facing up, close your eyes, and let your body totally relax. Rest three to five minutes.

32 thirtytwo

TOTAL RELAXATION

- *This time, relax on your back, arms at your side*
- *Close your eyes, rest three to five minutes*

Now to *#33, the Bridge.* After your rest, bend your knees, place your feet flat on the floor and bring them up as close to the buttocks as possible. Then, bring your arms up over your shoulders, elbows bent, fingers pointing toward your feet. Then, try raising your body up off the floor, putting your weight on your hands and feet. Hold for a count of ten, building to a count of sixty. This one will also probably take some time for many people. If you can't raise your body off the floor, just lift the buttocks up, resting your weight on your feet and shoulders. Continue to work the posture without strain. Whatever you can do is perfect for you at the time. Rest after this posture.

33 thirtythree

THE BRIDGE

- *(1) Bend your knees with your feet flat on the floor*
- *(2) Bring your feet as close to the buttocks as possible – bring your arms up over your shoulders, elbows bent, fingers pointing towards your feet*
- *(3) Raise your body up off the floor.*
- *(4) With practice, you will be able to arch your back.*

thirtyfour

Note:
This posture is performed laying on your back
NOT standing up

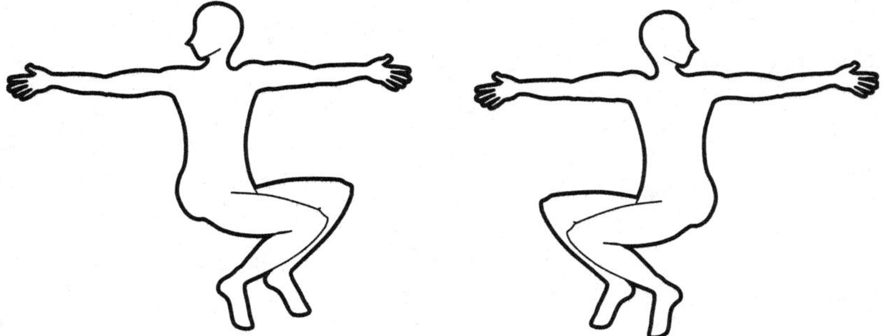

KNEE ARM STRETCH

- *Start by laying on your back*
- *Stretch your arms out straight from the shoulders keeping them on the floor*
- *Bend both knees and bring them up to the chest*
- *Roll the knees in one direction and the head in the other, bending at the waist*
- *Return to center and roll the knees in the other direction while moving the head to the other side*
- *Repeat two times on each side*

Next, go to ***#34, Knee Arm Stretch.*** From your resting position on your back, stretch your arms out straight from the shoulders, keeping them resting on the floor. Bend both knees and bring them up toward the chest. Roll the knees in one direction and the head in the other, bending at the waist. Look to the outstretched hand. Then, reverse the position, moving the legs to the other side and the head in the opposite direction. Repeat this posture two times on each side.

35 thirtyfive

MODIFIED HEADSTAND

- *(1) From a kneeling position, clasp your hands together and put them out in front of you*
- *(2) Angle your elbows out, resting them on the floor, creating a triangular cradle for your head*
- *Place the top of your forehead within the triangle formed by your hands and forearms*
- *(3) Lift your buttocks into the air, putting your weight on your arms and head*
- *At first, hold for as long as is comfortable.
Then hold for a count of 30, eventually reaching a count of 120*

Then go to ***#35, Modified Headstand.*** From a position on your knees, clasp your hands together, bend your elbows, and put your hands and arms on the floor in front of you, making a cradle for your head. Now, place the top of your forehead on the floor within the triangle formed by your hands and forearms. Lift your buttocks into the air, putting your weight on your arms and head. For beginners, come down as soon as you feel the need. As you continue with this posture, hold it for a count of thirty, building to a count of one hundred and twenty. When you are ready to come down, simply bend your knees, and roll over onto your back without taking your head off the floor.

This brings us back to ***#36, Total Relaxation.*** Relax for at least a couple of minutes before getting up.

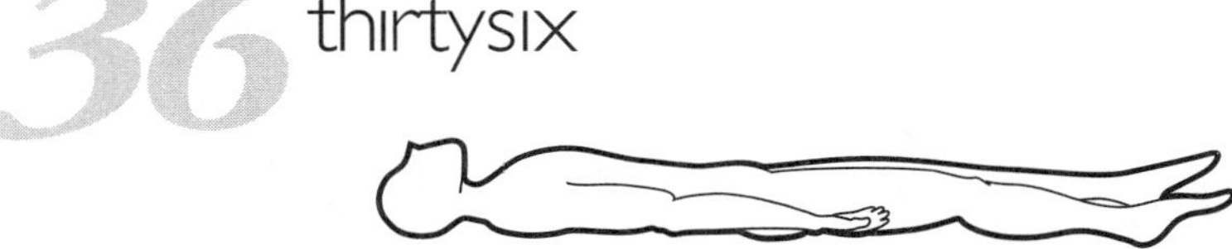

TOTAL RELAXATION

- *Relax for at least a couple of minutes before getting up*

This concludes *the Energizers*. This set of exercises works on all areas of the body to release stress, strengthen the nervous system and refine the mind/body energy, thereby preparing us for higher and higher levels of health and wellness. These energizers are a part of the preparation of the mind/body energy which allows us to tap into our intuitive abilities.

Sometimes people tell me they simply do not have time to do all of these exercises. It is not about time, it is about beliefs and choices.

Sometimes people tell me they simply do not have time to do all of these exercises. ***It is not about time, it is about beliefs and choices.*** They find that when they make a choice to do this process, they seem to *actually have more time*. A strong nervous system allows you to do less and accomplish more in the same time frame. When your body and mind are functioning better, it takes less time to accomplish the same tasks.

They find that when they make a choice to do this process, they seem to actually have more time. When your body and mind are functioning better, it takes less time to accomplish the same tasks.

After doing this exercise routine, your body is prepared for the next step—another breathing exercise then meditation, all described in the next chapter.

Twelve 12

Meditation

In silence, a being is identified with its pure freedom, with that pure possibility of itself, which it discovers when it retires within itself.

—Gisele Brelet,
twentieth century French writer

The next step in developing our ability to create the life we want for ourselves is training the conscious awareness to connect with who we are on a deeper level—to learn how to merge our conscious mind with the superconscious. This is accomplished through meditation. As an example, remember the circle with a dot in the center. The circle represents the ordinary mind which is busy constantly thinking thoughts. In other words, the mind is going around and around the circumference of the circle. If we can teach it to slow down and stay focused on one point, it begins to move toward the center of the circle—the superconscious, the source of all intelligence and energy. When we merge the conscious mind with the superconscious on a regular basis, the conscious mind begins to expand, and we experience a *knowingness* about the laws of nature and how we create our own experiences.

When we merge the conscious mind with the superconscious on a regular basis, the conscious mind expands and we begin to experience a knowingness about the laws of nature and how we create our own experiences.

There are a number of ways to meditate, and I will describe six methods for you to choose from. I recommend that you try all of them and choose the one that works best for you. We meditate after doing each set of our energizers—once in the morning before breakfast and then in the evening before dinner. The exercises prepare the body to settle down for meditation. We will begin with short forms of meditation, but once we become adept at it we will meditate for twenty minutes twice a day.

Before we begin our meditation, we want to do another breathing exercise. This is called the balanced breath. This breathing exercise balances the energy in our bodies, allowing the entire mind/body system to relax and settle down in preparation for meditation. In Eastern Terms it is called the balancing of the yin and yang, or in other words, the integration of the masculine and feminine energies *(see drawing on the next page).*

1 one

BALANCED BREATH

- *Women use their left hand – men use their right hand*
- *Cover one nostril with your thumb and INHALE through the open one*
- *Release nostril – cover the other one with your second and ring fingers*
- *EXHALE and then INHALE through the open nostril, now close the other nostril with your thumb and EXHALE – continue the process for two minutes*

Use your right hand if you are male, and your left hand if you are female. Close off one nostril with your thumb, and breathe in through the other one. Now, release your thumb and close off the other nostril with your second and ring fingers. Exhale through the open nostril. Now, inhale through the same side, close the nostril on the other side with your thumb again, and exhale. Continue this process for two minutes once you have mastered it. For beginners, do whatever feels comfortable for you.

The purpose of meditation is to transcend the intellect, to go beyond the thinking process and merge with the source of everything found at the level of pure silence.

The purpose of meditation is to bring the conscious mind to the level of the superconscious, or, in other words, to transcend the intellect—to go beyond the thinking process and merge with the *source of everything* found at the level of pure silence. We can use any of the physical senses to help us reach this level of silence. The idea is to focus our attention on one point. When we can get the mind to stay focused on one point, it automatically starts moving back to silence.

1. *Focusing Your Breath Meditation*

In this first technique, we will start by simply focusing your attention on your breath. Sit comfortably in a chair or in a crossed-leg position with something supporting your back. The idea is to be very comfortable, so as not to be distracted by your body. Place your hands in your lap, close your eyes and begin to focus your attention on your breathing. Breathe comfortably, as you usually breathe. Notice the breath as it comes in, bringing it all the way down into your abdomen. Then, slowly exhale, keeping your attention on your breath all the time. If thoughts slip in, as soon as you are aware of them, simply bring your attention back to your breath. Continue this process for three to five minutes. Notice the clock before you start, then again afterwards. You will soon be able to sense the right timing without using a clock. Do not set an alarm of any kind to measure your meditation time. The entire nervous system becomes very settled—an alarm will jar the system causing stress. When the time is up, slowly open your eyes and come back to outer consciousness remaining quiet and still for a few minutes before returning to your activities.

Be very gentle with yourself in all of the meditations. Never try to force anything, and do not get caught up in an argument with yourself.

2. *Focusing Your Sight Meditation*

After using the above technique for a week, let's work with another kind of meditation using the sense of sight. Select an object that you enjoy looking at. It could be a vase, a figurine, or anything else that pleases you. Place it about three feet in front of you. Sit in a comfortable position, and focus your attention on the object. Try to simply *be* with it for about three minutes. The idea is not to think about the object, but to simply observe it. Notice how often your mind wanders onto other things. Don't be distracted by these thoughts, and don't try to force them out. Simply bring your attention back to the object when you discover that you are off onto other thoughts. Observe how this technique works for you.

3. *Candle Concentration*

Prepare for meditation in the usual way, then place a candle in a holder that will catch the melting wax, and light it. Place it about three feet in front of you, on the same level at which you are sitting. Now, look at the flame of the candle and keep your focus on it for about two minutes. If the mind wanders just return your attention back to the flame. After a couple of minutes, close your eyes and bring the palms of your hands up to cover them. Look for the flame with your eyes closed. You will most likely detect the flame in some form. Just *be* with it. If you lose the image, just bring it back by continuing to look for it. Begin by practicing for another two minutes eventually expanding to twenty. Now, reflect on your experience.

The ordinary mind is accustomed to having its way, and will resist being disciplined, but in time it will learn.

Observation is a very important tool in discovering who we are and how life works. Be very gentle with yourself in all of the meditations. Never try to force anything, and do not get caught up in an argument with yourself. *You* have all the power. Even though old habits may not die easily, simply bring your attention to where you want it to be, and continue to do this as many times as is necessary. The ordinary mind is accustomed to having its way, and will resist being disciplined, but in time it will learn.

Another technique you can use with the sense of sight is to simply bring your attention to focus on anything in your surroundings. It could be a spot on the floor or wall. You can practice it any time, like when you are waiting in an office or for an elevator. What we are doing is teaching the mind to be able to focus. As we move into creating the things we want in our lives, you will see the value of this. It is the strength and clarity of our thoughts that determine the speed of our manifestations.

4. Music Meditation

Let's use the sense of sound for focusing our attention. Select a recording of some music that you particularly like. It needs to be music only, no words, and something that makes you feel good, not excited. After finishing your energizers and the breathing exercises, lie quietly on your blanket or sit in a comfortable chair. Play your music for about five minutes. Do not think about the music—simply experience it. Let yourself be an instrument through which the music plays. If you have thoughts that come in, just return your attention to the music. Gently release the thoughts whenever they arise.

5. Inner Sound Meditation

Most people have more success in their meditations when they use one of the techniques that utilize sound. I was using the inner sound technique when I had my first experience of profound knowingness and understanding of the laws of nature and how they work. Prepare for meditation as usual. Sit comfortably with your spine straight, arms and hands on your lap. Close your eyes, completely relax, and listen for a sound that comes from within yourself. The mystics say this is *the sound of creation being created*. People describe the sound differently. To me it is a humming sound, although some describe it like the distant waves of the ocean you hear from a seashell, and to others it is a "ringing" sound. Whatever you hear is fine. Most of the time when we start listening, we notice outside sounds first. As we continue to focus, we will connect with this inner sound. Once we connect with it, it can become quite loud. Since this inner sound is much closer to our source than outer sounds, once we connect with it, it is easy to transcend and merge with pure silence. It's important to note that even the slightest experience of pure silence brings great benefits.

All these techniques for meditation are simply tools for training the conscious mind to merge with the superconscious. Our goal is to blend with the silence and access the unlimited energy within us.

Each time we meditate we merge with the silence—the source of all sound, energy and intelligence. These experiences have an accumulative effect. This is why we need to meditate twice a day, every day. Each time we merge our conscious mind with the superconscious we return with an expanded awareness. We make better choices, and begin to understand how the creative process works through the laws of nature. Changes start to take place in our lives. We cannot explain it, but we simply begin to intuitively know whatever is necessary in any given situation. Meditating on a regular basis is how we develop this intuition. The longer we work with the process the more we experience this *knowingness* until it becomes an integral part of our everyday lives. Eventually, we can hardly even remember what it was like living any other way.

All these techniques for meditation are simply tools for training the conscious mind to merge with the superconscious. Our goal is to release ourselves into the silence. We use the meditative tools and techniques that work best for us as the means to reach this goal.

6. *Mantra Meditation*

Next, we will discuss mantra meditation. A mantra is simply a word or thought used for focusing our attention on one point, preparing us to journey inward. There are many mantras or sounds that we can use. Sometimes someone will ask me, *"Why can't I just pick a word, and use it as a mantra?"* The sound of the word we use as a mantra is very important. And since the sound of a word and its meaning are so interrelated, it would be ineffective to choose a word that didn't have the appropriate energy. Different sounds have different effects in the energy fields. The Transcendental Meditation movement has made mantra meditation popular. There have been numerous scientific studies done on this form of meditation, and the findings have shown outstanding benefits for its practitioners. A TM teacher initiates a person into the practice of meditation and gives him/her a mantra that is specifically selected for this person following a set of specific criteria. These sounds have no given meaning since a meaning could distract you from quieting your mind. You can find transcendental meditation centers in most major cities. I used TM for many years and found it very valuable. In addition to teaching meditation,

A mantra is simply a word used to focus our attention on a single point, preparing us for our journey inward.

the movement also provides other personal and spiritual growth opportunities.

The mantra "OM" is used frequently. This is also said to be the sound of creation being created. Using this mantra in a group can be a very powerful experience. If you would like to try it, sit with your back straight, just as in all other meditations. Take a full deep breath. Then, make the "O" sound as you exhale half the breath. Make the "M" sound with the remaining breath. Do this seven times, then sit quietly and notice if you can feel the vibration of the energy around you. It can also be used as an internal sound if you are practicing your meditation in a space where it is not appropriate to speak out loud. The experience will be different, but still powerful. And as we know, the more subtle the vibration the more powerful it is. We just are not as consciously aware of it.

If you should fall asleep during your meditation it just means that you need more sleep. Your system is not capable of maintaining awareness right now. When you wake up and realize that you have been sleeping, simply go back to your meditation. It's all OK.

The mantra we have selected for our use is the word "Love." Since the sound of a word and its meaning are closely related, "Love" is most appropriate. But when using "Love" as a mantra we are not focused on the meaning of the word—we are using it for the quality of its vibration. We simply repeat it over and over, and the vibration of this thought brings the conscious mind toward its source.

Now, let's try it. After completing a set of energizers and the balanced breath, sit comfortably with your back straight. Put your hands in your lap, close your eyes, let yourself settle down, then start thinking the word *"Love."* Think the word *"Love"* over and over in an easy manner, just as you would think any other thought. When you notice that your mind has wandered off onto another thought, simply bring it back to the mantra. As you repeat the mantra it may speed up or slow down. It doesn't matter. Just keep your mind focused on this one word or sound. The mind will eventually tire of the sound and automatically transcend and merge with the superconscious on the level of pure silence. This is the purpose of all meditation.

Meditation Review

1. We recommend that you meditate for twenty minutes twice a day. You might want to start with a ten-minute meditation, but soon you will want to spend more time. In whatever way is comfortable for you, increase your meditation to twenty minutes.
2. Set a clock where you can see it. Notice the time when you start your meditation, then when it feels like the time is up, simply open your eyes and check the clock. If the time is not up, just close your eyes and continue meditating. Once again, do not set an alarm when you are meditating. An alarm will jolt the nervous system and create stress.
3. If you should fall asleep during your meditation, it just means that your body needs more sleep. Your system is not strong enough to maintain full awareness at this time. When you wake up and realize that you have been sleeping, simply go back to your meditation. If your allotted time is up, it is still good to return to the meditative state for a few minutes.

4. After meditation, sit quietly with your eyes closed for a couple of minutes, then slowly open your eyes and take a few minutes to bring your attention back to outer consciousness before moving.
5. Remember that meditation is about letting go of thoughts and bringing the conscious mind back to silence, its source. Choose the technique that works best for you, but set aside twenty minutes for meditation twice a day. The first thing in the morning is the best time for our full routine of breathing exercises, energizers and meditation. This prepares you to be at your best throughout the day. If you put this into your schedule every morning you will notice a great difference in how your day goes. Late in the afternoon, before dinner, is another perfect time to do the full routine again.
6. Every time you do the energizers, the breathing exercises and meditation, you release the stress that has accumulated in your body, and refine the mind/body energy. This enables you to intuitively know the laws of nature and make choices in harmony with them to create the life you want. When we do not have a program for releasing the stress on a daily basis, we simply go around and around the circumference of the circle. By functioning in the same old limiting ways, we create the same old things, never understanding why life happens as it does.
7. This process, when practiced on a daily basis, will lead you to an entirely new way of life. It will create better health on all levels, broaden your horizons, allow you to see many more possibilities and enhance your ability to live a life filled with peace, joy, happiness and fulfillment.

2 two

Beginning Movement

- *(1) Stand straight with the palms of your hands flat together – Salutation Posture*
- *(2) Observe that your posture is just the way you want it – clasp your hands together with your palms facing out and up, bring your arms over your head*
- *(3) Stretch to one side, then to the other*

Core Movement

- *(4) Bring your arms over your head, stretch back and* **INHALE**
- *(5) Bring your hands to the floor – support your weight on your legs and hands making an inverted "V" shape with your body – now,* **EXHALE**
- *(6) Bring your right leg up into a "runners" pose – look up and* **INHALE**
- *(7) Place your feet back together returning to the inverted "V" position and* **EXHALE**
- *(8) Bend your knees and lower your body to the floor*
- *(9) Bend your elbows and place your hands, fingers facing in, under your head – push back, keeping stomach on the floor and* **INHALE**
- *(10) Push yourself up into the inverted "V" position again and* **EXHALE**
- *(11) Bring your left foot forward, knee bent into a "runners" pose, look up and* **INHALE**
- *(12) Bring your foot back, returning to the inverted "V" and* **EXHALE**
- *(13) Bring your feet forward*
- *(14) Return to a standing position and* **INHALE,** *then breathe normally*

NOW, return to position 4 and use your left leg at position 6, continuing through to position 19

Completion Movement

- *(15) Salutation Posture (see Step 1)*
- *(16) Clasp hands together behind you*
- *(17) Bend backwards as far as you can and* **INHALE**
- *(18) Bend forward bringing your arms up as high as you can behind you and* **EXHALE**
- *(19) Salutation Posture*

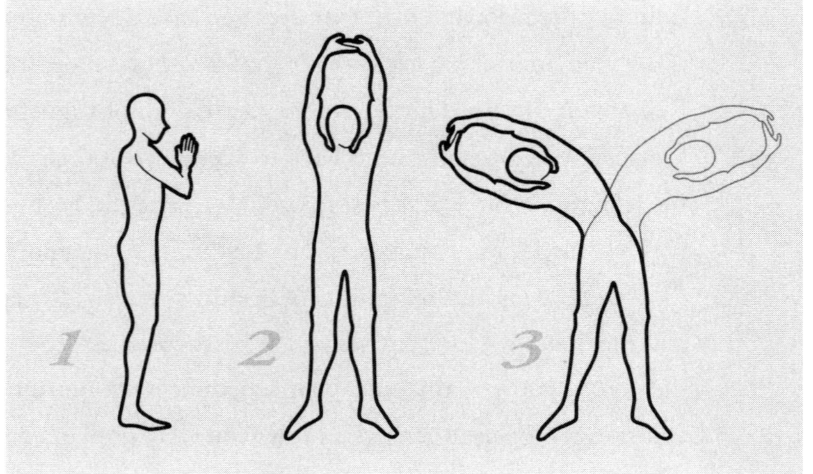

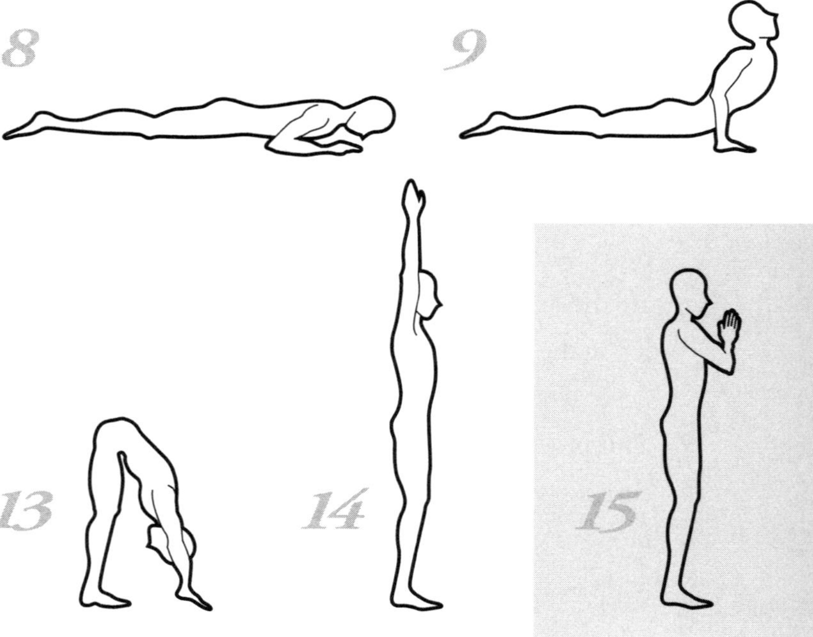

Salute to the Sun

Salute to the Sun

Here is one more stretching exercise. This single series of movements allows the body to fully relax with just one routine of stretches. If you cannot do a full set of energizers in your evening program, then you can substitute this routine to prepare yourself for meditation. It can also be used as an aerobic exercise in the morning (in addition to your regular full set of *Energizers*).

Beginning Movement

1. Start in a standing position with the palms of your hands together in front of you as shown in diagram 1 on *pages 142-143.* Be sure you are standing straight and that your posture is just the way you want it to be. This is called the *Salutation Posture.*
2. After observing your posture, bring your arms up over your head, clasp them together, palms facing upward and stretch as high as you can.
3. Then, stretch to one side and then to the other, as far as you can without pain.

Core Movement

4. Now, bring your arms up over your head, palms facing out, stretch back a little and INHALE.
5. Bring your hands down to the floor, supporting your weight on your hands and feet, making an upside-down "V"-posture with your body and EXHALE.
6. Next, bring your right leg up, knee bent, into a "running" pose. Look up and INHALE.
7. Bring your feet back together, returning your body to the upside-down "V"-posture and EXHALE.
8. Bend your knees and lower your body to the floor.

9. Now, bend your elbows and place your hands, fingers facing in, under your head and push back, keeping your stomach on the floor and INHALE.
10. Next, push yourself back up into the inverted "V"-posture and EXHALE.
11. Now, bring your left foot forward, knee bent, into a "runner's start pose". Look up and INHALE.
12. Bring your foot back, putting your body into the inverted "V"-posture, and EXHALE.
13. Put your weight on your hands and bring your feet forward.
14. Now, bring your body up straight and INHALE and return to normal breathing.

Now, repeat the Core Movement one more time, this time alternating legs, starting with the left leg instead of the right one. Do the Core Movement as many times as six sets if you choose.

Completion Movement

15. Finish the routine by bringing the hands, palms together, in front of you, while standing with a straight, perfect posture.
16. Extend your arms behind you and clasp them together.
17. Bend backward as far as you can and INHALE.
18. Now, bend over to the front as far as possible, bringing your arms up behind you as high as you can and EXHALE.
19. Then, finish with the Salutation Posture.

The *Salute to the Sun* movement is also a good exercise for concentrating on the breath. You INHALE when the head is up and EXHALE when it is down. You may need to follow the chart the first few times you practice this exercise, but in time you will remember, and it will simply become a part of your daily routine.

As mentioned before, the *Salute to the Sun* routine can be used in two different ways. First, you can perform the movement in place of your evening set of energizers if you do not have the time to complete a full program. You can also add it into your morning energizer routine as an aerobic exercise.

1. ***Substitution for a full set of energizers***

   To prepare for meditation when you cannot do a full set of energizers, perform the routine from position #1 through position #14 *(see chart on pages 142-143).* Then, go back to #4 and repeat the entire Core Movement again, starting with the left leg instead of the right leg. After reaching position #14 the second time, move on to position #15 and end with the Completion Movement.

2. ***Added in with your energizers***

   When using this routine with a full set of energizers, it fits in after you have finished *the Bicycle* and rested—between Energizer #4 and #5. If you would like to use this routine as an aerobic exercise you may repeat the Core Movement up to six times—three on each side. Start with #1 *(see chart on pages 142-143),* being observant of your posture before beginning. Follow through to #14, then return to #4, and use your left foot instead of the right for the next set. Continue this, alternating the starting leg each time. After six sets, finish the Completion Movement with postures #15 through #19.

Now that you have discovered a twice-daily routine for releasing stress, strengthening the nervous system and refining your energy—you have started the process for developing your creative and intuitive abilities. In the next chapter we will start working with the *Seven Steps in the Creative Process.*

Thirteen

The Seven Steps in the Creative Process

The mind is eternal in so far as it conceives things under the form of eternity... From this kind of knowledge arrives the highest possible peace of mind, that is to say, the highest joy, attended moreover, with the idea of one's self.

—Benedict Spinoza, seventeenth century Dutch philosopher

In chapter 7 we introduced the seven steps in the creative process. It is now time for you to begin using them to create whatever you choose.

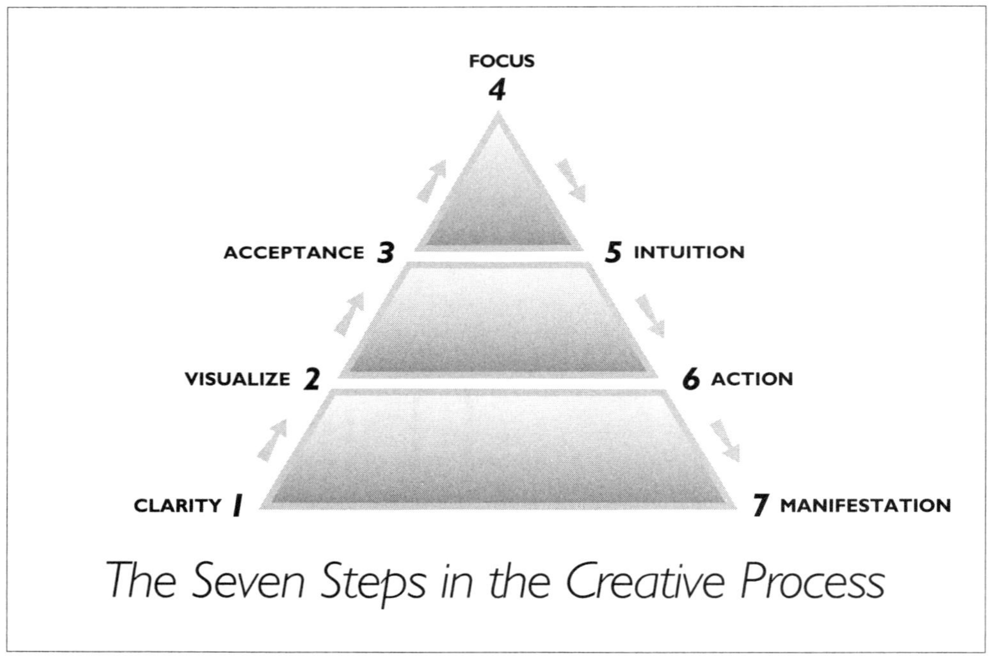

The Seven Steps in the Creative Process

Above is what we call the seven steps in the creative process. We must work through each of these steps in this order to create our choices. We have set it up in the form of a triangle to help you to more clearly understand how the process works. *Clarity* and *Manifestation* are the foundation—the beginning and the end—with *Focus* being the capstone. If we were clear about what we wanted to create and focused our attention on it, it would manifest. However, this takes a higher degree of concentration than most people have. Understanding, and working with the other steps makes the process much easier. Let's look at each of the seven steps separately to discover the role of each step in creating our choices.

Step 1 — Clarity
Taking the time to KNOW what you REALLY want

You will need a notebook for working with this process. You will be writing very personal things in this notebook, so be sure to keep it in a private place.

Choices

1. Start with a fresh sheet of paper and write a summary of where you are in your life right now. It is only for you, so be perfectly honest and describe as fully as you can all the different aspects of your life at the present time. When you have finished, put this paper in the back of your book. Later, you can go back and read it and see how your life has changed as a result of working with this process.
2. Take another clean sheet of paper and make a list of seven things that you like about your life. Then, make another list of seven things that you do *not* like about your life.
3. On a third sheet of paper make a list of seven things that you would like to create in your life. They can be anything that you desire—concrete or abstract—the only requirement is that you will be able to recognize it when you have manifested it.

Here are examples of some things that you may want to create: personal habits or characteristics, inner peace, a special relationship, a fulfilling career, a new skill (playing the piano, becoming a gourmet cook, improving your game at tennis), material things such as an automobile, a boat or a house. You get the idea. It can be *anything* you want in your life. You can start by reviewing the things that you do not like about your life and decide to change these things. Or you can just write down whatever you desire.

We work with a list of seven because that is about as many as you can focus your attention on at one time. As you manifest these choices, you can cross them off your list and add others.

Remember, you are now beginning to create your life the way *you* want it to be—not what someone else wants for you, or what you think you are *allowed* to have. It is very important to ask yourself, *"What do I want?"* Take a break from reading the book and write your list now.

STOP

WORK ON YOUR LIST OF PERSONAL CHOICES NOW

---

4. After you finish your list, look at it again and ask yourself, *"If I created this today, could I accept it?"* If you can honestly answer "YES" to each item, re-write the statements inserting *"I choose"* at the beginning of each sentence. You are making a choice to create these things in your life—making a commitment. The subconscious needs to clearly understand this level of commitment. *Choosing* is more determined than *wanting*. To *want* something is very passive. You can want something forever.

Here are some guidelines for making your choices:

a. Write the result you are looking for, NOT how you think it can be done. Focus your attention on what you want, NOT on how you are going to make it happen.

b. Write in the present tense, as if the thing you desire already exists.

c. Be sure to write what you want, NOT what you do not want.

d. Do NOT write down what you think you *should* want. When you re-read your list, if something does not excite you, remove it.

e. Do NOT make choices for other people. For instance, you can choose the *kind* of relationship you want, but not the specific person you will have the relationship with.

5. Go back over your choices and be sure they follow these guidelines. For instance, if you made a choice that reads something like: *"I choose to make a good impression at work so I will get a promotion,"* your statement violates Guideline "a". You would want to change your choice to read something like: *"I choose to create a position for myself that I love, which gives me an opportunity to express myself and pays $__________ (insert the amount) which I am worth and deserve."* The main point here is to get as clear as possible about what you want and describe the result you are looking for. Do not give a second thought as to how it will happen. Universal Intelligence knows how to create it. Your job is just to get *clear* about what you want and *know* that you *can* and *will* create it. How you will create it will be revealed to you as you go along.

A statement such as, *"I choose to take a nice vacation sometime soon,"* violates Guideline "b"— *write in the present tense.* First, it is not specific enough about what you want and, secondly, it is not written in the present tense. You would want to change this choice to read something like: *"I choose a vacation in the Virgin Islands."*

An example of a choice that violates Guideline "c" would be something like: *"I choose to lose weight,"* or *"I choose to get out of debt."* Here you place your focus on what you do *not* want—excess weight and debt. These choices need to be changed to: *"I choose to create a healthy, lean, firm, beautiful body for myself,"* or *"I choose to create the money I need to pay for all the things I choose to have in my life."*

Do not use these examples as your choices. Your choices need to be exactly what *YOU* want. These are just ways to help you understand how to work with the guidelines. Next, let's look at Guideline "d". If you have a choice such as: *"I choose to get a job that will please my mother,"* instead you need to ask yourself, *"What do* I *want?"* In actuality, you can't know what will really please your mother. You have no control over what others like or dislike. Your job is to get clear about what *you* want.

Another violation of Guideline "d" would be: *"I choose to have Bill/Susan fall in love with me."* You get to make all of the choices about your life, but so does everyone else. Bill/Susan gets to choose who he/she falls in love with. When you understand that you are in charge of your own life, you will begin to see that you have no need to make choices for others. You can create exactly the kind of relationship you want, so change your choice to something like: *"I choose to have a close and intimate relationship with someone I love and who loves me."*

We have been working with this process for many years, and thousands of people have taken our course. It is amazing to see what happens when people actually apply these principles in their lives. In one class, a lady who was in a marriage that was not to her liking asked if there was any way she could change her husband. My answer was, *"You can only make choices for yourself,"* at which point she replied, *"OK, I am going to create the kind of relationship I want whether it is with him or not."* She then created her vision of the kind of relationship she wanted. In a few weeks she reported that she could not believe how her husband had changed. She said, *"He is turning into my ideal mate."* Did he change or did *she* change? I don't know. I can only tell you that Universal Intelligence brings us whatever perfectly fits our deepest beliefs and expectations. This is why it is extremely important to get as clear as possible about what we want in our lives. What we believe on a deep level clearly determines what we will attract into our lives. Again, we get what we believe in and focus our attention on.

Creating Basic Choices

You now have a list of seven things that you want to create for yourself and they are written according to the guidelines. We call them—*Main Choices*. Now, we make a different kind of choice.

Basic Choices

I want you to make five choices we will call your *basic choices.* These choices build the foundation we need in order to create our main choices. These choices are so basic, you might have already covered some or all of them in your main choices. If so, you will be able to add some more main choices to your list.

- ***Basic Choice 1—Choose to love yourself.*** *What does it mean to love yourself?* Give this some thought. One of the things that comes to mind for me is to take care of myself—do my program, eat right, exercise, and maybe enjoy something special like taking a bubble bath. My understanding is that Love is who we are, so maybe it is taking the time to really get to know yourself. What you want to find out here is what this means to you. Take the time you need to get clear on this for yourself.
- ***Basic Choice 2—Choose to choose.*** In order to create the life you want you must take charge. You must take full responsibility for your experiences. It is valuable to realize that it is YOU who makes all your choices. Choose to take charge of your life and create it the way you want it to be. Again, it is important to take all the time necessary to understand what this means to you.
- ***Basic Choice 3—Choose health—physical, mental, emotional and spiritual health.*** *If you were totally healthy in all areas of your life what would it be like?*

Things that come to mind for me on the level of physical health is feeling fully alive, full of energy and vitality. Every cell is vibrant and intelligently playing its role in the proper functioning of the entire body. Mental health might mean being clear and sharp, alert and knowledgeable. Emotional health could mean feeling stable, secure, loved and loving, able to laugh and cry and experience all aspects of life. My definition of spiritual health is feeling whole and complete, connected with my source, knowing that I am not separate, but at one with all. It could be the awareness of the love and power that resides within all. These are just some thoughts on health. Take some time and find out by asking yourself what it means to be healthy in all these areas. If you are choosing to be healthy, you will need to be able to recognize it when you have manifested it.

- ***Basic Choice 4—Choose freedom.*** *What does it mean to be free? If you were totally free what would it feel like? Who keeps you from being free?* Again, take the time you need to discover what this means to you. Many times we believe that others keep us from being free. We now know that it is we, ourselves, who make all the choices in our lives. If you are feeling less than free in any area of your life you might want to consider making some different choices. Again, remember that this whole process is about taking charge of your life and creating it the way you want it to be.
- ***Basic Choice 5—Choose to be true to yourself.*** *What does it mean to be true to yourself?* One of the things that comes to mind for me is to refuse to do anything that conflicts with my values. *Does being true to yourself have anything to do with honesty?* First, we want to be totally honest with ourselves, and when we are, we can be totally honest with others. Again, explore this choice and see what it means to you.

Once you have worked through these five choices put them at the top of your list of choices. Committing to these five choices makes it *possible* for us to create *all* our other choices.

- You now have written your choices and organized them in your notebook. You will be working with these choices every day. You need to read them every morning to set up your day. Every evening, you will want to spend some time to *work* with them. Refine and update your choices as new insights comes to you. As we become more and more aware of what is truly important to us, our choices and priorities change. Remember, nothing is set in stone. Any of your personal choices can be changed. People have changed entire lists. When you work with your choices every day, you will certainly get new insight about them and become clear about what you *really* want in your life.

What you will soon see, as you continue to work with this process, is that your choices will begin to manifest. You will get whatever you have chosen, so you want to be very clear about exactly what you want. Remember, everything is energy and we are working with the law of attraction and repulsion. Whatever you place your attention on *will* attract the energy necessary to create whatever you have chosen, and repel other energy that is undesirable.

It is also very valuable to remember that if you have not worked on changing your beliefs to be in harmony with what you want to create, your deepest beliefs will show up. When my husband Dean created his ideal position, he forgot to get clear about what kind of boss he wanted. He ended up creating a boss very much like his dad since that was the only boss he had ever worked for. If you aren't clear in your mind about what you want, whatever has been programmed into your subconscious will appear in your creation.

Step 2—Visualization
Allowing your choices to live and grow in your creative mind

The next thing we need to do is visualize what we want to create. Visualization is very easy. We all do it all the time. If I say *"Think of a pink elephant,"* what happens in your mind? Usually, you automatically create a mental picture of a pink elephant. In fact, it is almost impossible *not* to do it.

Sometimes we can create a *photographic* rendering in our mind. Other times we generate a *word picture* or a *feeling sense.* It is all the same—they are each different ways to experience a mental visualization. When we create a vision, this picture in our mind *creates* a form. The law of attraction will then pull the energy necessary to fill this form into our lives. This doesn't happen instantaneously, but as we live with a vision we intend to have manifested, the law of attraction begins to work. Our intention plays a major role in this process. This is why we preface each of our choices with *"I choose,"* as an indication of intention and commitment.

Practicing Visualization

1. Let's begin this process by picking a practice choice. Choose one of your choices to begin working with.
2. In your mind's eye, create a picture of something you would see when your vision is manifested. This does not have to be a still picture—it could be like a video clip.
3. Use as many of your senses as possible in creating this vision.

For example, if you wanted to create a new car for yourself it might be beneficial to go to a car dealership and check out the car you are interested in. Here you are, impressing all of its features in your mind. In creating your vision—see the car with all of the options you want—admire the body and the interior, imagine the colors you want. Smell that *new car* smell. Feel the steering wheel in your hands, and bring it out on the road for a test drive. Hear the wheels sing along the pavement. The idea is to create the experience of *having* your new car. In your mind it is *already* yours. Be sure to put yourself in it and sense what it feels like to have this car. You are creating the *form* that will attract the *energy* necessary to bring this new car to you. Remember, we first create the form in our minds and then the law of attraction takes over and things start to happen to bring about what we are experiencing in our minds to the physical level of our awareness.

4. Now, create a *SECOND* picture of something that you will see when your vision is manifested. You might see yourself showing your new car to a friend. Again, use as many senses as possible in creating this vision.
5. Finally, create a *THIRD* picture of something that you will see when your vision is manifested. Make your choice a part of your life on the mental level. It is just amazing to see how circumstances and events change to bring your visions into material manifestations when you hold clear images of them.

Let's try another example of a different choice. If you wanted to create a life partner you might imagine what he/she looks like. Envision his/her personality. Sense how he/she feels about you. You would include everything that is important to you in this vision of the ideal mate you are creating for yourself. See the two of you together. What are you doing? If anything shows up in your mind that you do not want, immediately discard it and replace it with what you *DO* want in this person. Use all of your senses in visualizing this ideal partner and your relationship with him/her.

As described above, you will want to take some time to create at least *three* visions for *each* of your choices. Do not rush. You should be able to sense when each choice has become a part of your intention and expectation. There is a very peaceful feeling that comes over you when you have been able to fully accept your choice.

Step 3—Acceptance
Knowing, working with, and changing your beliefs

Acceptance. This should be easy, right? Actually this is the most difficult step for most of us. This is where your beliefs come in. It's amazing how many of us don't believe that we can *actually* have *anything* we want *without making apologies to anyone.* We have all kinds of reasons and carry lots of beliefs about why we can't have one thing or another. It is important to know—we will only manifest what we can accept. The tricky part here is that we are not consciously aware of about eighty-five percent of what we believe.

A process for changing your beliefs

1. The first step is to become consciously aware of your beliefs.
2. Take a clean sheet of paper from your notebook and make a list of anything that comes to mind that could possibly keep you from creating any of your choices.

We have all had a tremendous amount of programming about how things work and what's possible. Most of us have been given even MORE information about what's *im*possible. Remember that ***beliefs are only information that we have accepted as truth,*** and that we become very attached to our beliefs. The challenging part is that most of what is generally accepted as truth is not true at all. **This means that MOST of us need to change MOST of our beliefs**—a fair amount of work. But this may just be the most rewarding work that you have ever done for yourself in your life. There are no absolute truths except for the laws of nature. When something can be true in one set of circumstances, but not in another—this is a relative truth. We are taught to believe that most of our relative truths are absolute and that if something is true in one situation it will also be true in another. This allows us to get through life without much need for thinking, but rarely creates an ideal experience.

3. Take your list of limiting beliefs, which will all be of a negative nature, and change each one into a positive belief—one that will coincide with the laws of nature we have been working with. Here are some examples of beliefs programmed into our psyches:

a. "Money doesn't grow on trees"—meaning that you do not have enough money for what you want (and most-likely never will).

b. "There's only so much I can do"—meaning that there are pre-set limits to what you can accomplish.

c. "You can't have it all"—meaning you must choose between financial success and personal freedom.

d. "Life's a hard row to hoe"—meaning that success is the result of hard work.

Are these statements true? No. They are actually all false. Just because money doesn't grow on trees it doesn't mean that you will not have as much money as you need. Money is energy, and ***thought directs energy.*** We create lack in our lives only when we believe in it. Now, let's look at "b". *What determines the limits of your accomplishments?* Your own thoughts create these limits. Consider "c". *Can you have financial success and personal freedom?* Of course. You only need to *choose both.* Think about "d". *What precedes action?* Success is actually the result of clear thinking followed by efficient and informed action. Activity is an important part of life, but remember that action *follows* thought. In order to be successful in anything, we first need to get in touch with our beliefs, and change them if they are not helping us to fulfill our choices.

4. Take all the time you need to work with this exercise. It is vitally important to get in touch with your beliefs. We cannot change beliefs until we are aware of them. Beliefs can only be changed on the *conscious level* of consciousness.

5. Go back over the summary of your life. Review the list of things you do not like having in your life. Ask yourself what beliefs you are holding that create these experiences. Your life is, in fact, a perfect expression of your beliefs.
6. Make a list of all the things that could be causing you to create what you do not want in your life.
7. Now take these lists of beliefs and write the truth about them as we did in the examples. Remember, ***beliefs are only information that you have accepted as truth.***
8. This is a technique which we call *"Reject, Reverse, Replace."* When you discover any belief that is not beneficial in helping you to create what you want—*Reject* it. Tell yourself that this belief is not true, and you will not continue to believe it. *Reverse* the direction in which this belief has been taking you. *Replace* it with the truth about the situation. Create a new belief that supports you in your growth and success. Since it is simply information, accept only positive information that helps you to create what you want. Remember that you are an expression of Love, Intelligence and Energy. You are an integral part of a perfect system, discovering how to live in harmony with it.
9. Becoming aware of our beliefs is a continual process of observing our thoughts. Once we make this commitment, it is amazing to see how clearly our beliefs show themselves. Our thoughts and beliefs create our experiences. Through the law of attraction and repulsion these beliefs provide us with an exact replica of whatever we believe. As we change our limiting beliefs, our life experiences will change to match them.

Next, let's take a look at what your beliefs say about you. Many people in our lives, beginning with our parents, have had opinions about us, and they usually openly related those opinions to us. We have either accepted or rejected their opinions—thus determining to a great degree how we see ourselves. These opinions have either aided or undermined our self-esteem.

10. Think back over your past and bring to mind what the people in your life have said to you about who you are—your abilities, your failings, your talents or lack of abilities. Write them all down. Now, change them to be what you want to create for yourself.

11. We now want to create an ideal self-image. Close your eyes and see yourself being the person you are choosing to be. Now, say your name, and every time you close your eyes and say your name, become this ideal person.

You can see why the acceptance step is the most difficult for most people. It requires time, probably the rest of our lives, to work with our beliefs and become able to accept the lives we want for ourselves. However, when we continue to use these techniques on a daily basis, we continue to make progress—every-single-day.

Another major aspect that we want to understand is that our beliefs are a part of the electromagnetic energy field which makes up our mind/body system. As we continue to do our energizers and breathing exercises, and meditate on a daily basis, the stress and negative energy is released from the mind/body system. This allows us to automatically become more confident and be able to change our beliefs to become more positive and life supporting. We also are automatically expanding our awareness experiencing how the laws of nature work together on all levels. It is almost impossible to change our beliefs without first healing and strengthening the nervous system. As our energy becomes more refined, our ability to see things from a different perspective increases.

Step 4—Focus
Being responsible for placing your attention on what you want

The experiences we bring into our lives are whatever we focus our attention on. Nothing exists for us until we acknowledge it by giving it our attention. This attention brings energy to the object of our focus allowing us to experience it. Few people understand how this principle works, much is lost due to a lack of attention.

The following is an example of this principle. When I met my husband, he was looking for a position in the business world. He had worked in the family business and had been in private practice, but he had never actually applied for a job. He had a huge résumé that was quite impressive, but when I asked him what he wanted to do, he didn't actually know. He mentioned more than ten different possibilities. I explained the *focus* principle to him and showed him how his attention was scattered all over the place. He wasn't able to give any of these different visions enough energy to manifest. Dean needed to get clear on what he wanted and commit his focus to *one choice*. As mentioned earlier in the book, he created an ideal vision of exactly what he wanted to do, and then manifested the vision. Part of the process was focusing his attention on his vision every day.

Another example is a very bright, energetic woman I knew. She was obviously very talented, and was involved in a number of different ventures. In fact, she seemed to be trying to go in so many different directions at the same time that none of her ventures paid off for her. How could it be that she was so busy, and had so many different possibilities, but nothing actually worked out for her? It wasn't a lack of talent or ability. It was a lack of focus. Her energy was splintered, and she was not directing enough energy in any one direction to bring it into being.

Understanding this principle helps us to realize the power we have in our own lives. If we focus enough attention on something, it will surely manifest. On the other hand, if we ignore anything it will disappear.

Practicing how to focus your attention

1. Reserve a block of time for focusing your attention on your choices. This is the reason why we work with only seven at a time. This is about as many things as we can give sufficient attention to in order to bring them into being.
2. Go back and look at your choices. Many times when we work with them for awhile, we realize that we can combine some of our choices, and actually make our list smaller. This is good. The smaller the list the more attention you can give to each one. In fact, it could be helpful to work with only two or three choices at a time. Select the ones that are most important to you and start there. Remember, you can mark them off your list once you have manifested them, and you can also add others.
3. I recommend working with (focusing your attention on) your choices twice a day. The first time, simply bring them into your awareness. The second time will require more time. Read them over and notice if you have any new insights about them. Reassess their level of importance to you, and see that they are stated as clearly as you can get them. Review the *Choices Guidelines* on *page 148* and make sure that your choices meet all the criteria.
4. Next, expand on your choice. Write using as much detail as you can see. You will actually want to have two lists of choices—one written as succinctly as possible for quick shots of attention (energy). The other list should be written in as much detail as you can imagine for use when you have a longer period of time for visualizing them.

5. Next, visualize the manifestation of your choice using three different mental pictures. This is focusing your attention on your choice and giving it energy.
6. After completing this, notice whether you have any resistance to accepting the full manifestation of your choice. *Are there any negative thoughts that crop up?* If so, work through the process for changing beliefs.

As you focus on your choices every day, you will soon notice circumstances and events occurring to help bring your choices into fruition.

Step 5—Intuition
Connecting your conscious mind to the superconscious mind

This is where our listening skills come into play. Most of us do not know how to listen. We get so caught up with what is going on in our lives that we have a hard time hearing what other people are saying to us. We always have something important to say. Have you ever caught yourself interrupting someone, forcefully expressing your own opinions before they even had a chance to finish talking? Have you ever become anxious, impatiently awaiting your turn to talk to the point of not actually hearing what the other person is saying? *If we can't even listen to others, how can we hope to hear the very subtle voice of intuition?*

Our inability to listen is a result of an over-stressed nervous system. As we release the stress built up in the system through the practice of the energizers, breathing exercises, and meditation, we become more settled. A feeling of calmness and peace begins to emerge. We feel less pressure to talk, and begin to learn how to listen. As we continue to work with this process on a daily basis our ability to listen increases, and soon we begin to hear the inner voice of intuition.

Observation is the perfect tool to help us measure our progress. Do you still find yourself pushing to get your opinion into a conversation? When someone disagrees with you, do you actually hear their point and consider it before replying? When we have released enough stress, which keeps the mind/body energy heavy, our *energy* becomes more refined and intuition is an automatic result. We must become settled, quiet and peaceful in order to connect with clear intuitive awareness.

How to use intuition to work with questions

1. Intuition, like everything else, comes to us when we focus our attention on it. So, let's start by thinking of a question. It should be a question that is important to you. It should require more than a yes or no answer. Write your question on a clean sheet of paper in your workbook.
2. Now, close your eyes and use one of the forms of meditation that we learned in *chapter 12* and meditate for a few minutes. Then, let go of the meditation technique, and ask your question. Open your eyes and write down the first thing that comes to you after asking the question. If it doesn't make any sense, write it down anyway. Try the same process again the next day.

Some people start with getting pieces of the answer they are seeking. After working with the process every day, information begins to come together and starts to make sense to them.

This process teaches the mind/body system that you are open to intuitive guidance—that you expect to get it. What happens after practicing the energizers, breathing and meditation techniques for a period of time is that you simply begin to know. Intuition becomes a part of your life, and questions are no longer necessary. You will begin to automatically know whatever you need to know, and your life becomes one of *right action* which brings about the desired results.

Distinguishing Between Intuition and the Intellect

Intuition is different from a thought or belief. Intuition is simply a *knowingness.* It is very difficult to describe, and we must experience it for ourselves to truly understand it, but I want to give you some guidelines for distinguishing the difference.

A woman in one of my classes called me and was very upset. She thought she had received something intuitively that frightened her. First, we need to understand that intuition is not attached to any emotion. If you get something that is frightening, the information is definitely coming from the intellect. Intuition comes from the level of wholeness. Anything of a negative nature is simply the absence of the awareness of this *wholeness.*

Intuitive awareness is not a thought, it is just awareness. We simply know something, and we have no doubt about it. We *know that we know.* It does not come from any logical determination. If someone asks, *"How do you know?"* we cannot explain it. Intuitive awareness just comes to us. My experience is that we receive intuitive awareness about things that are very important to us. When I ask a question I usually get an answer, but sometimes I don't. To me this means that I really do not need to know the answer right now, or that I will be guided to discover the answer in another way when the time is right. Intuitive awareness is always there for us, but we must learn how to become quiet and still and tune into it.

Step 6—Action
Taking the human footsteps that bring in the manifestation

Once we become intuitively aware of what we need to do, we simply follow through with the appropriate action.

Action is easier for us because it is an outer process, and we are familiar with it. We are constantly *doing* things because this is the only way we know how to fulfill our desires since so many of us are not consciously connected with the fourth dimension—the spiritual dimension of ourselves. Now that we have become aware of how the entire creative process works, we see action from a different perspective. It is simply a follow-through process after we have completed the five previous steps. Many of the problems we face are because we enjoy taking action so much that we don't take the time away from it to discover what needs to be done and why. Without consciously moving through the first five steps of the creative process, taking random action only depletes our energy and leaves us frustrated.

How to take action consciously

1. Get very clear about what you want to create. Visualize it as being complete and perfect. Accept it fully and ask for intuitive guidance. NOW is the time for your action step, it is time to follow through with the appropriate physical activity.
2. We must be willing to do our part. What is done for us is usually *done through us*. Universal intelligence will guide us once we have developed our ability to receive it—to listen to it. When we learn how valuable this guidance is, universal intelligence will send us more. Many times we will not be able to see why we are guided in a certain direction, but once we have learned to trust our intuitive awareness, we go with it. Then, in time, it will all unfold for us and we will be able to see it clearly.

There is always some action that must take place, but your action needs to come from a place of clarity. We are accustomed to acting without a clear understanding of why we are acting in the way we are. By using this process, our actions become much more powerful than what we usually experience. Once we act, we then let it go for universal intelligence to carry out the correct consequences and unfoldment of our desires. We do not *make* things happen, we *let* them happen.

Step 7—Manifestation
Receiving the gift of your creation

Actually, manifestation is more of an occurrence than a step in the process. We include it as a step because we need to pay special attention to how it works. When we complete the first six *Steps of the Creative Process,* manifestation is the result. We manifest whatever we have chosen to create.

If we manifest something that is not to our liking, then all we need do is retrace the *Steps of the Creative Process* and see what's out of balance. First, is our mind/body refined enough to create what we want? Are we clear about our creation? Have we spent the necessary time visualizing the results? Are we willing to accept what we want? Which of our beliefs are functioning? What are we *actually* focusing on? Have we asked for intuitive guidance? Did we follow through and *act* on the guidance? When we manifest something different than what we *say* we wanted, we often have instead manifested a belief hidden away in our subconscious mind. We can just continue working the tools of creation and re-focus our attention on what we want.

Most times, we are delighted with what we manifest, but since this process works over time, the intellect often has a hard time following it. Therefore, the manifestation step is about becoming aware of how the entire process works. By the time our visions are manifested we have totally accepted them, and if we are not observant we can think they just came *out of thin air.* It is important to understand that it is *not just another experience* and realize how our manifestation came to be.

The manifestation step is one of appreciation, joy and gratitude for the ability we have to create the lives we want for ourselves. It is about becoming more and more aware of the process so we are better prepared for our next creation.

14 Fourteen

My New Lifestyle

If we live truly, we shall see truly. It is as easy for the strong to be strong as it is for the weak to be weak. When we have new perception, we shall gladly disburden the memory of its hoarded treasures.

—Ralph Waldo Emerson

Morning Routine

1. Wake up after a full night's sleep. After your bathroom trip, (which includes brushing teeth) go outside (or at least get your head out into the fresh air) and do your purifying breaths.
2. PURIFYING BREATHS—Take a deep breath in through the nose, bringing the air all the way down extending the abdomen while filling the chest. Then, forcefully exhale out the mouth. This fills the lungs with fresh air and releases the stale air that accumulates in the lungs overnight. Do this only three times.
3. Spread your special exercise blanket in your designated place for doing your program. Sit in the center of it. Work with some deep breathing for a couple of minutes. Place your hands on your stomach and feel your abdomen as it fully extends. Then, start your massage toward the heart.
4. Continue with the full set of energizers.
5. After completing the energizers, sit in a comfortable, crossed-leg position with your back straight and supported. Do the balanced breath for two minutes. Have a clock where you can see it.
6. Now, close your eyes and meditate for twenty minutes.
7. After meditation bring to consciousness one of your choices and visualize it as fully accomplished. Then, open your eyes and read through your full list of choices.

Evening routine

1. Do a full set of energizers, or, if time is a factor, do *Salute to the Sun* as illustrated at the end of *chapter 12*.
2. Meditate for twenty minutes.

3. Then, before opening your eyes, ask a question for which you want an answer *(see chapter 13 on how to work with questions).* Open your eyes and write down the first thing that comes to you.
4. Visualize the full manifestation of one of your choices.
5. Sometime before bed, take at least thirty minutes to read over your list of choices, visualize them and update them as new insights come to you.

Things to observe and make choices about in your daily life

If we do not learn how to be conscious about the things that are happening in our lives, we simply react through our programming and function like robots. When we do this we give away our power to consciously create whatever we want. We all have strong programs about how life is *"supposed"* to be. We know how a woman is *supposed* to act, and what a man is *supposed* to think. We know what a good wife and husband are *supposed* to be like. We've been told about the qualities that are *supposed* to make you a good parent. And how children are *supposed* to behave. We know how friends and neighbors are *supposed* to treat us. We have ideas about how a business is *supposed* to run and our government is *supposed* to function. We have beliefs about everything in our lives.

No one knows just how long it will take for our visions to manifest. As surely as the seed we put in the ground will produce a plant if we keep it watered, so will our our visions manifest. We keep them watered by focusing our attention on them, staying available and willing to do our part.

What we are usually unaware of is how we came to these beliefs in the first place. Most of these thought patterns have been repeatedly reinforced into our thinking by other people, including friends and family, teachers and clergy, the media and our government, and others who like to be seen as experts on a particular subject. Many times these people have a vested interest in convincing us to believe as they do. We rarely take the time to consider the beliefs we hold. It is now time to consciously start making *belief choices* for ourselves.

When something upsets you, ask yourself:

1. Which of my beliefs is being threatened?
2. Is this belief helping me create what I want in my life?
3. How important is this belief to me? Why? When we get upset we damage our health. Is maintaining this belief really important enough for me to want to damage my health?
4. What am I thinking and saying while I'm upset?
5. Is what I'm thinking and saying in accord with what I want to create in my life?
6. Am I *condemning, complaining or criticizing* someone or something, including myself? Does this have any value? Will this help create the life I want?
7. What kind of energy must I be putting out in order to create this upsetting experience? Remember the law of attraction—***what comes from us returns to us.***

Personal observations to make on a daily basis

1. Observe your body. Is it relaxed?
2. Is your mind focused on what you are doing?
3. Notice how you are affected by the people in your life. If friends with negative energy leave you feeling drained, you might want to find new friends. It is a good rule of thumb to associate with people who have as much life force as you do or more.

4. Notice how you are affected by the entertainment that you engage in. When you see a movie or TV show, or when you read a book, magazine or newspaper, for all practical purposes you are experiencing whatever you are focusing your attention on. Are these the kinds of experiences that you really want in your life?
5. Observe how stress affects the people around you. People can behave in radically different ways when they are over-stressed. Notice the stress in your life and how it affects *your* behavior.
6. Observe how much of your life is in the present moment. When we are thinking about the past or the future, we are missing the present. Life is now—we can only live in the present.
7. Notice if you find yourself rehashing old events or conversations. One of the most valuable things we can learn is that when something is over, it is over. There is nothing more that we can do about it. As it becomes part of the past, we need to let it go and move on with our lives.
8. Are you willing to experience whatever is? We can spend days, weeks, even years, dreading something that we fear might happen. The minute you decide to experience whatever is, you are freed. A great technique to practice is to consciously let go of your resistance and *be* with whatever is. What you will find is that your thoughts about something and the actual experience of it will be quite different.
9. Notice how well you receive. It is our beliefs that block our ability to receive. ***Become a master receiver.***

We rarely take the time necessary to deliberately explore the beliefs we hold. It is now time to get conscious, and start making belief choices for ourselves.

10. Practice using your ideal self-image technique on a regular basis. Simply say your name to yourself and become the ideal self that you created earlier.
11. Observe your diet. Do you overeat or drink? Is your food fresh? How do you feel after eating?
12. Observe the role of exercise in your life. Do you exercise on a regular basis? Walking in the fresh air at least thirty minutes a day can be very helpful.
13. Notice your breathing throughout the day. At first, just observe how deeply you breathe. Do you take short, shallow breaths—or measured, deeper breaths? Take some moments out of the middle part of your day to practice deep breathing.

Three-month Check-in

Here are some things to do after you have been practicing the energizers, breath exercises, meditation and observation techniques for at least three months:

1. Review the life summary you wrote when you began this process. *How much has your life changed?* We use this exercise in our course and most people notice dramatic changes taking place. One woman once said, *"I do not even know this person that I have written about any more."*
2. If you feel you need to more clearly understand your purpose in life, ask to know your purpose after your meditation, before opening your eyes. Ask this as you would ask any other question and work with it in the same way. Write down whatever comes to you and keep asking the question until you feel that you are clear about the answer.

3. Now, take some time, as much as you need, to think about the life you would like to create for yourself. Write the story of your life. You can write in the third person if it is easier. Make your personal story exactly the way you want it to be. Have some fun with this! Now, visualize your new life unfolding for you, and accept it. Make a commitment to yourself—create this life. Work with the Seven Steps in the Creative Process to ***create your life JUST the way you want it to be.***

Our creations always go through a process. The first part of the process is when we create our visions. This is fun and we are very excited—but then comes the germination phase. This is the unseen part. It is like planting a seed. We cannot see anything happen for what seems like a long time, but then the plant begins to sprout. The same is true with our creations. There is a time when our visions are taking root, when all the things that are necessary to manifest our visions are taking place, but we cannot see them. This is a time for patience and not a time for doubt. If we doubt, it is like digging up the seed to make sure nothing is going wrong. This would disturb the rooting process and you would have to start all over. No one knows how long it will take for our visions to manifest, but just as surely as the seed we put in the ground will produce a plant if we keep it watered, so will our visions manifest. We only need to keep them watered by keeping our attention focused on them and be willing to do our part.

If you follow this routine on a daily basis it will lead you through a transformation process which leads to self-actualization. In the next chapter we will see how this process unfolds.

Fifteen

15

Transformation

Of all the knowledge, the wise and good seek most to know themselves.

—William Shakespeare

Just as the caterpillar must go through a metamorphosis to become a butterfly, we must also go through our own transformation to become self-actualized. In our caterpillar state, or in the state of ordinary consciousness, we have only the use of the conscious and the subconscious minds. We are limited to the information provided by the senses. In this state, our life consists of memory, beliefs, judgment, ego, personality, thinking and problems. We can live our whole lives on this level.

However, it is a choice. Just like the caterpillar, we can go through our own metamorphosis. By doing the program laid out in this section on a daily basis, changes start to take place. The mind/body energy is refined, enabling us to release the stress stored in the nervous system and merge the conscious mind with the superconscious. This strengthening of the system allows us to expand our awareness and change our beliefs or programming, thereby making it possible for us to create proper functioning throughout the entire mind/body system. This new way of functioning refines the energy of the entire system so it begins to resonate with the energy of the superconscious. As you remember, the superconscious is the level of all knowledge, the source of intuition.

Choosing to go through a personal transformation we come to a state of self-actualization. Fully realizing our potential, we enjoy intuitive guidance in all that we do. Our daily lifestyle brings us in contact with universal intelligence—ALL knowledge and Love.

Choosing to go through this transformation brings us to self-actualization. As a self-actualized person we enjoy intuitive guidance in all that we do. Our daily lifestyle brings us in contact with universal intelligence—all knowledge and love—and our everyday realization of our oneness with all. Some of the results that we usually experience are optimal health, happiness, joy, enthusiasm, compassion, success and wealth—spiritual, cultural and material.

In most cases we also get a clear sense of purpose. We all have a shared human purpose—which is to grow into self-actualization and mastery. We each also have a special gift to share with the world around us. When we are in touch with this purpose and are living our lives *on purpose*, we feel totally fulfilled. It need not be something that appears to be spectacular, but it *is* important and only *you* can fulfill this purpose.

Every one of us can choose this new lifestyle and create an expanded life for ourselves. *How might this new way of functioning unfold in* your *life?* I could write another book on the experiences of people who have participated in our classes and how it changed their lives. They have healed themselves of heart problems, cancer and numerous other ailments. Many have also created new businesses and lives far more fulfilling than they could have ever imagined. Your experiences will depend on what you want and your level of discipline in following the guidelines.

Some of the results that we usually experience are optimal health, happiness, joy, enthusiasm, compassion, success and wealth—spiritual, cultural and material.

What I want to do here is to give you an example of the benefits that come from committing to the process and making it a part of your life. With her permission, I would like to share with you some of the experiences Joan Gustafson has had as a result of this program. Joan was introduced to our *Unlimited Futures* course by a fellow executive at 3M Corporation. He shared with Joan the many benefits he had gained from the course in both his personal life and in his ability to make a contribution to 3M.

People have healed themselves of numerous physical ailments, created new businesses and built lives that are far more fulfilling than they could have ever imagined. Your experiences will depend on what you want and your level of DISCIPLINE in following the guidelines.

She came to the course with three major goals in mind. First, she wanted to create a compatible, loving partner with whom to share her life. Second, she wanted to build her dream house. And third, she wanted to expand her responsibilities and influence within 3M.

Joan had been dating Cliff for several months, but the relationship didn't seem to be going anywhere. Cliff came to the introductory session with her, and he also decided to take the course. As it turns out, he had suffered a heart attack, and Joan was very worried about a possible recurrence. They both learned the power of thought, and they began to see Cliff as perfectly healthy. This removed Joan's fear, which was creating a gulf between them. Cliff's health improved, their relationship grew stronger, and they were married the next year.

She had placed her house on the market when she came to the course, but it wasn't selling. She had found the land where she wanted to build her dream house, but couldn't start the project until her present home was sold. She began visualizing the house selling and the new one being built. She visualized it in detail and within a few weeks a cash offer came in on her house. She moved into an apartment and began building on the property with the lovely pond she had found.

Joan also decided what she would like to do with her career. She created a vision of a new department at 3M. Before the three-month class was completed, she had been offered the opportunity to do exactly what she had created in her mind. She was able to select the people for this new department, and she chose wisely. It was a great group of individuals. One of the first things she wanted to do was introduce her new department to our *Executive Development Program*. We held a half-day workshop for all of them, and at the end of the session everyone decided to sign up for the program. She had invited her boss to this session, who also chose to participate in the course.

The Unlimited Futures Executive Development Program helps individuals become all they can be and gives them the ability to make significant contributions to their organizations. Employees who function at a higher level of creativity provide the organization with a greater level of success.

Our *Executive Development Program* was provided in four two-day sessions held once a month in a special conference center. She had ten managers in her new department which was the perfect size for our program. They all came and experienced outstanding results. This group of employees made significant contributions to 3M, and have created more fulfilling personal lives for themselves as well.

Joan's next goal was to create an international position for herself. She had decided that she wanted to expand her new department into Europe. She was told that international assignments were almost nonexistent at the time. This, of course, didn't faze her. She knew how thought and visualization works to create your desired outcome, so she simply continued to focus on her vision. Joan worked the seven steps in the creative process, and within a short time, the opportunity she had envisioned appeared.

We all have our own dreams and we can make them come true by making a commitment to use the techniques in Part Three of this book.

Cliff was a chiropractic doctor, and he was able to sell his practice in the exact time frame they needed to make the move. They were in Europe, based in Paris, with a beautiful house in the countryside for two years. Joan traveled all around Europe working with different 3M offices, and Cliff came along for the adventure. She accomplished her business objectives and they had a great time during their two years in Europe, just as she had envisioned.

Joan has now taken early retirement from 3M and has written *A Woman Can Do That!—Ten Strategies for Creating Success in Your Life,* a book designed to help women become more successful in the business world. She and Cliff have built a beautiful new house in Arizona for their semiretirement. Joan started her own business, providing seminars and workshops. Her company is *"Success and Leadership Dynamics."* Her slogan is *"Opening doors to brighter futures for individuals and organizations."*

As a result of practicing the program laid out in this section Joan has taken charge of her life and is creating it just the way she wants it.

You have your own dreams and you, too, can make them come true by committing to develop *your* ability to understand and live in harmony with the principles of life that we uncovered for you in this book. Work with the *Seven Steps in the Creative Process* and create your life just as you choose it to be.

16 Sixteen

A Dozen Questions

Questioning is one of the most valuable things we can do for ourselves. We need to understand what things mean to us and how they will work in our life.

—Dr. Bobbie Stevens,
twenty-first century psychologist and futurist

Simply spending time with the concepts in this book can begin an amazing process of discovery for you. But information alone is not enough. Life is about experience. This is more than a book filled with fascinating information—it is a practical step-by-step *HOW TO Guide* directing you to become self-actualized *yourself!*

You can take deliberate action, today, that will start bringing you the life you have been dreaming of. You can have greater health, happiness, rewarding relationships and a renewed sense of connection to Source and the world around you.

It is about a totally NEW way of living—a new way of thinking—a new way of focusing your time and talents. It's a new way of looking at *everything* in your world. This chapter deals with the most important questions that our participants have asked over the years. These answers will help set your expectations and begin to create a level of commitment so that you can create phenomenal success.

Q ONE — *What are the basic steps of the* Unlimited Futures *method?*

1. You have already completed the first part—opening your mind to the idea that *YOU* can *actually* create any life you desire for yourself. Making a *commitment* to the program and process outlined in *Part Three* of the book is the *most important step.*
2. It is valuable to understand and begin to embrace the qualities of a self-actualized person. Review *Chapter Four* and know that these qualities are already inside you.
3. Become familiar with the *Seven Laws of Nature* as outlined in *Chapter Five*. There are many laws, but these seven work together to provide a strong foundation for your continued personal growth and change.

4. Focus on four vital activities of awareness:
   - look at everything in the world as ENERGY,
   - know the negative impact that STRESS has on your mind/body system and your *ability to create*. Make it a priority to consciously release as much stress as possible everyday,
   - work with your BELIEFS knowing that they are the building blocks of your life experiences,
   - practice making more conscious CHOICE
5. Commit to the program of *Energizers* as presented in *Chapter 11*
6. Become aware of how you breathe and practice the breathing exercises in *Chapter 11*
7. Embrace a discipline of *Meditation* as detailed *in Chapter 12.* Through this practice, you connect to Universal Intelligence through your intuition.
8. Work the *Seven Steps in the Creative Process* as outlined in *Chapter 13* to bring all aspects of the *Unlimited Futures Program* together in order to create whatever you want.

Q TWO — *You talk of the PROGRAM— what is involved on a daily basis?*

1. *Stretching Exercises*—a series of physical exercises called *Energizers*. Specifically chosen because they activate the energy centers in the body, they help the nervous system release stress allowing your mind/body system to heal and become more refined.
2. *Breathing Exercises*—these are practiced along with the *Energizers* and connect the mind with the body, helping energy to flow properly through the mind/body system.

3. *Meditation*—allows the mind to settle down so that it can merge with the super-conscious (all intelligence), and bring back to the conscious mind an expanded awareness.
4. *Focusing on our Choices*—is the time set aside where we work with the *Seven Steps in the Creative Process* to create anything we want for ourselves.

The daily program includes all four of these disciplines. The first three will take approximately one hour to complete. Then you decide how much time you want to spend focusing on what you want to create for yourself.

Q THREE — *The Program sounds powerful, but time consuming. Is there a way I could just take "baby steps"?*

If you are looking to take "baby steps", you have missed something along the way. It is desirable to get to a more advanced way of functioning as soon as possible. Taking "baby steps" will just delay your progress. What you will discover as you release stress and strengthen the nervous system is that you are able to do less and accomplish more. We have been programmed to live our lives in a certain way, but we are simply doing things the hard way. We must be willing to let go of the old way of functioning to discover a better way. We cannot expect to keep doing the same old things and get a different result. This process is about creating a new lifestyle for yourself. Once you make a full commitment to this new way of living, you will discover that life simply doesn't work the way you thought it did. You will start seeing great new possibilities and exciting ways of pursuing your goals.

So, it is certainly *not* about taking "baby steps"—it is about taking "adult steps". You can not know it until you *experience* it. Start working the program today and you will be amazed with the changes that begin to take place.

Q FOUR — *What makes your program different than others in the market?*

I am not familiar with all of the programs in the market—I can only tell you that this process works. Since 1984, we have not found a single person who did not grow tremendously from practicing the techniques outlined in this book. Participants have shared with us their ideas on what makes the *Unlimited Futures* program different and one of them gave us this description.

He explained that other courses were very dramatic filling him with excitement. But, as life went on, what he had learned became less and less valuable to him.

Personal impact from many other courses

The *Unlimited Futures* program, on the other hand, was quiet. It was not a *rah, rah* thing. But he found, as time went by, its impact continued to grow and provided more and more practical value to his life.

Personal impact from Unlimited Futures

Unlimited Futures is the only program that I am familiar with that understands and works with the main underlying reason why we are *unable* to create what we want for ourselves:

- Until our nervous systems are strong enough to allow the necessary changes to take place for the manifestation of our choices, what we want remains just dreams or desires outside our grasp.
- The *Unlimited Futures* process is specifically designed to strengthen the nervous system so an individual is strong enough to *let go of the old* and *make room for the new.* With an over-stressed system, one is simply *not* capable of seeing possibilities or creating new experiences. Our first focus is on releasing the stress that has built up over the years. After this happens, people automatically move into a much more advanced level of functioning and are capable of creating whatever they want.
- Information alone cannot bring us to this new level. Additional information, *without a process of releasing stress,* just creates more work for an over-stressed nervous system.
- As the nervous system becomes stronger and healthier, our ability to manifest our choices actually increases. This is another reason why the *Unlimited Futures* program has such a great accumulative residual effect.
- The process outlined in this book is 99% experiential. It is *not* an intellectual pursuit. You must *work* with the process for it to work for you.
- The program is successful for ***anyone*** who commits to it and makes it a part of their lives. It requires *both* commitment and discipline to be able to enjoy the results.

Q FIVE — *Aren't the Energizers just yoga? Can't I get the same results from my current routine?*

Most of the energizers are yoga postures, but they have been specifically chosen and put in an order that will stimulate the energy centers, release stress from all parts of the body and mind—strengthening the entire mind/body system. For best results, follow the directions and illustrations found in *Chapter 11.* They should also be done twice a day, everyday, for the quickest and most desirable results. However, it is best to start wherever you can. Some people have a hard time making a full commitment all at once. Whatever you can do, will bring about some level of success. As you begin to see the changes in your life, it will probably be obvious that you will want to make a full commitment allowing your growth to be more complete.

Q SIX — *I go to the gym in the morning. What should I do first, my workout or my program?*

Do the *Unlimited Futures* Program first. It prepares you for the best results with your workout and a much higher level of effectiveness throughout the day.

Q SEVEN — *I can't seem to quiet my mind. I'm always thinking twenty different things at the same time. How will I ever learn to focus?*

As you work with this process on a daily basis, the entire mind/body system automatically becomes much more settled. The stretching exercises relax the body, allowing the mind to settle down for meditation. At the beginning, your mind may be rebellious and random thoughts may *come out of nowhere*. This is normal. Make a commitment to simply sit in meditation, regardless of what your mind is doing or saying to you. Once you take charge you will find that your mind will respond.

Q EIGHT — *I'm having financial problems. How will exercises and meditation put money in my pocket?*

Most financial problems are the result of stress that block one's perception, and the limiting beliefs you hold around money. As stress is released, the mind becomes clearer and you are able to see possibilities you couldn't see before. The increase in energy that comes from practicing the program on a daily basis also gives you the very energy you need to pursue these new possibilities. It is extremely *freeing* to understand that life doesn't work the way we've been taught and that you now have new ways of creating what you want.

Q NINE — *I want to make a lot of money. Will the program help me do that?*

Absolutely—*Money is energy,* as is everything else. However, if you want money, the first question you need to ask yourself is what you want it for, since money is just a means of exchange. You will need to work with the first step in the creative process until you are very clear about what is *really* important to you. Then, explore the beliefs you have around money. Everything is energy and we can discover how to form this energy to create whatever we want. When you get clear about money, you can create it just as you can create anything else.

Q TEN — *I have some health problems, how can this program help me?*

The *Unlimited Futures* process is about healing. This change in life style can make a huge difference in your body's ability to function properly. Most health problems are a result of the built-up stress in the mind/body system. As this stress is released, the body begins to heal and strengthen itself. We certainly do not claim that this is a cure for anything, but over the more-than-twenty years that we have been providing this course, we have seen people heal themselves of most every health problem that exists. It is all about choice and commitment.

Q ELEVEN — *I'm in my seventies and have arthritis, I won't be able to get down on the floor to perform the Energizers. What do I do?*

Start the process by doing whatever you are physically capable of *without* straining—then *visualize* yourself doing the rest of the postures. What you visualize is recorded in the sub-conscious and positively affects your physical health. People from 16 to 90 have participated in our courses and all have benefited tremendously.

Q TWELVE — *I would love to share this with my partner, but he/she is not interested, what can I do?*

As you know from reading the book, you are responsible for your *own* well-being. You cannot make choices for others. Usually, when one partner works with the process and starts creating positive results, the other partner becomes much more interested. All you can do is be true to yourself and discover how it all unfolds.

Q BAKER's DOZEN — *I've been working the program and I'm delighted with the changes in my life. Are there any follow-up sessions that I can participate in?*

Yes, we provide *Personal Growth and Development Courses* for your continued growth. These are in-residence courses that allow you to remove yourself from your daily activities and take some time where you can dedicate yourself to deep rest, releasing stress, gaining more knowledge and getting clear about what you want to create for yourself. They are always held at beautiful locations and there is time set aside to enjoy walks in nature and a unique opportunity for you to connect to yourself and like-minded individuals. For more information on these courses please visit our web site at *www.theufb.com.*

Having a STRONG nervous system is the key!

Most of us believe that knowing *how* to do something is all that is necessary. But, we must also be *capable* of doing it. How successful we are at *doing anything*—including working with the *Seven Steps in the Creative Process*—is determined by the condition of our nervous systems. Just living in the world today almost assures that we are over-stressed. When our nervous systems are overwhelmed, our ability to become clear about what we want is diminished. It becomes difficult to visualize and it is almost impossible to observe and change our beliefs. Most everyone in our society today suffers from a form of attention deficit disorder, not just the children. Few people can stay focused on anything for very long. If we are unable to focus our attention, then it is obvious that we will not become quiet enough to listen for our intuitive guidance. When we are not really capable of working the first five steps in the creative process, the action we take is just *spinning our wheels.*

You CAN take charge of your life and create it the way you want it to be, but it requires that you work with the process for releasing stress and strengthening your nervous system ***on a daily basis***. As you work with this process of stretching exercises, breathing exercises, and meditation, your ability to work with the seven steps will dramatically improve along with your ability to be successful in creating the life you want for yourself.

In the first three sections of the book, we have given you the background, the theory and a detailed daily program that you can use to become a self-actualized person. Next, let's look at what could be different—in your life and the world around you—as more and more people become self-actualized.

PART
FOUR

4

What's the Difference?

Introduction

In this section we want to see what difference it would make in all areas of our lives if we became self-actualized. I will use the word "ordinary" to describe the person who is functioning with the use of only the intellect and the five senses, which is true for the majority of us.

The self-actualized person has the same intellect and senses as the ordinary person, but they also have the ability to tap into what I call the *fourth dimension*—the spiritual dimension—of life. Knowledge from this dimension is brought to the conscious mind through intuition. From this level of knowledge we are able to perceive the laws of nature that govern our lives and the material world. The self-actualized person sees situations from a different perspective than the ordinary person, and consequently, will act in a different way.

Each chapter in this section will explain the differences in a specific area of life. I will select situations that I believe are common to most of us in our personal lives, our relationships, and in business or the workplace. In the last chapter, we will look at how our society could change as more and more of us become self-actualized.

17

Seventeen

What's the Difference in Personal Experience?

In as much as the Soul is present, there will be power.

—Ralph Waldo Emerson

Subject *Self Image*

How do you feel about yourself? For the ordinary person, how we feel about ourselves is determined primarily by what *others* think of us and the feedback they give. The ordinary person allows other people to affect his perception, and regularly seeks the approval of others.

The self-actualized person enjoys approval, but does not need it to feel good about himself. He understands that we are all connected. He knows that everything is energy, and that his thoughts are subject to the law of attraction and repulsion. It is his *own* thoughts about himself that determine what others think about him.

Subject *Time*

Do you have enough time? The ordinary person believes that time is limited, and often feels pressured and anxious about getting things done on schedule. The self-actualized person knows that time is eternal. There are twenty-four hours in every day for each of us. He realizes that it is he, himself, who creates ALL the time frames in his life. If he has created something that doesn't work well for him, he can choose a new time frame or open up to different expectations. He realizes that his own thoughts and beliefs have created the situation he finds himself in, and he can change these thoughts and choose something else. The self-actualized person knows that he is in charge of his life and it is up to him to create whatever he wants.

Subject *Survival or Work*

Do you work to survive? How do you feel about your work? The ordinary person believes that he must work to survive—to make the money necessary to fulfill his needs. In this case, the amount of money a specific profession pays is a major factor in determining what work he pursues. And when the ordinary person is out of work, he probably will feel a great deal of stress and anxiety.

The self-actualized person works just as the ordinary person does. However, he does not believe that his work is essential to his survival. He knows that he is part of a perfect system that puts him in the right place, at the right time, in order to fulfill his purpose in being here. He knows that we are all parts of this perfect system—guided by universal intelligence—to bring about whatever is necessary for the growth and fulfillment of the whole. He sees his work as an opportunity to express himself. He knows that his desires and the *fulfillment* of his desires come from the same source. Consequently, he cannot have a desire without also possessing the means to fulfill it. He trusts universal intelligence and is therefore relatively unaffected by being out of work. He sees it as an opportunity to move on to something new which will inevitably bring him greater growth and satisfaction.

The self-actualized person's work is usually something he enjoys doing. He knows that ***thought directs energy,*** so he always *expects* his work will be to his liking. In fact, he expects only positive experiences. Since we usually find what we are looking for, even if an experience, like losing a job, comes into his life, the self-actualized person sees it as positive.

Subject *Money*

Do you have enough money? The ordinary person believes that he must make money to provide for his needs. They never have quite enough money to fulfill their desires. This makes it very important to accumulate money even without having any clear idea of what money really is. There is just a feeling that *more is better.*

The self-actualized person knows that money is simply a means of exchange. He does not feel compelled to make money. He knows that money is just another form of energy, as is everything in existence. Understanding that ***thought directs energy*** along with the ***law of attraction and repulsion,*** he knows that he can attract the money he needs when his thinking is clear and focused. This does not mean that he does not work—it simply means he sees the situation from a different perspective. Some self-actualized people have large amounts of money, while others have very little. How much one creates is determined by the amount of money needed for what one wants to do.

Subject *Judgement of Others*

Do you often judge other people and have strong opinions about the appropriateness of events and circumstances that do not involve you? The ordinary person likes to judge other people. He thinks that whatever amount of information he has about another person or their experiences is sufficient to make a judgment about it. Since we know that the intellect can only see parts of the whole, it *always* gathers incomplete information. Our intellect believes it knows everything necessary to make a judgment, and goes ahead.

The self-actualized person knows that the intellect is limited. It is incapable of having the information necessary to make valid judgments about another person or event. Therefore the self-actualized person simply accepts whatever he sees, and doesn't bother to judge it.

Subject *Anger*

Do you anger easily? How do you express your anger? When someone does something that seems threatening to us we usually become defensive. If we think someone is infringing on our rights, it provokes anger. How do you feel when someone in the car behind you blows his horn the second the light turns or follows too close behind you or cuts in front of you? For many of us, situations such as these trigger anger. If someone you know tells a mutual friend something negative and untrue about you, how do you feel? How do you handle it? Do you do something to retaliate?

The self-actualized person knows that we are not separate, but that we are a part of a whole perfect system. He knows that we are always putting out an energy that demands *"like"* energy in return. He also knows that he has a choice. He can either *react* to the energy that is being directed at him in the same way or he can choose not to be drawn into it and *respond* with a different kind of energy. As he becomes more aware of how energy works, he can simply choose to not get involved.

Usually the ordinary person is holding so much stress in the mind/body system that he is incapable of choosing not to become involved. When we are exhausted by the demands of our life, it doesn't take much to trigger our anger. In fact, we find ourselves getting angry about things that would not bother us if we were less stressed.

The self-actualized person is seldom over-stressed. He is aware of how energy works and the effects of an over-stressed nervous system. Consequently, he lives a lifestyle that allows him to release stress on a daily basis keeping his nervous system strong, thereby giving him the ability to choose not to become involved with destructive energy.

Subject *Power of thought*

How powerful are your thoughts? The ordinary person's mind is running constantly. He has so many thoughts going on at the same time that few of them are very powerful. It is usually a challenge to keep his attention focused on one thing for very long. Studies show that the attention span of the average person is quite short, and is actually decreasing. On the other hand, stress is increasing in our lives and is responsible for our inability to focus our attention.

The self-actualized person's thoughts are usually very powerful. He is capable of focusing his attention for a much longer period of time. He also has the ability to move to the project at hand regardless of what else may be going on. When our thoughts are clear and focused, they have a much greater effect on the energy field—

the source of energy that generates all the creations we are focusing on. Therefore, the self-actualized person has the ability to create whatever he wants in a much shorter time frame than the ordinary person.

Subject *The death of someone close*

How do you feel about death? The ordinary person is often totally overwhelmed by the death of a close friend or family member. Again, our beliefs and the condition of our nervous systems play a major role in how we handle the death of someone close to us.

The self-actualized person sees life as eternal. The death of someone close will be a sad occasion for him, and he will certainly feel the loss. But he will see it as though his friend simply moved away to a place where he can no longer see him. He will know that his friend still lives, grows and has experiences—appreciating that the love connecting them is never destroyed or diminished.

What's the Difference?

These chapters are designed to help us see the advantages of developing our potential for self-actualization.

The self-actualized person is not a saint. He or she make mistakes like everyone else. Life's challenges are still presented, and choices must be made. He is simply healthier, stronger and more capable of creating the life he wants. The self-actualized person has tremendous advantage over the ordinary person due to the development of their intuitive abilities to work with the laws of nature. With this comes the wonderful realization that no matter what happens, they can handle anything.

This, I believe, is what is called peace.

18 Eighteen

What's the Difference in Relationships?

This region of truth is not to be investigated as a thing external to us... It is within us... Consciousness, therefore, is the sole basis of certainty...

—Plotonius, third century Greek philosopher

Subject *Control*

How do you get others to see things the way you do? Control is a major issue that plagues most relationships. The ordinary person believes that we are all separate and have distinct minds of our own. This makes it necessary to explain how we plan to handle a particular situation and try to convince others in a relationship that our approach is the best (and sometimes the *only*) point of view.

The self-actualized person intuitively knows that there is only *one mind*, and we are all connected within that *one mind.* He also understands the ***law of attraction and repulsion.*** If he clearly knows what he wants, he will attract others into his experience which will make it possible for him to fulfill his desires. There is no need to convince *any*one of *any*thing.

The ordinary person thinks he has it all figured out and knows the specific people who should be working with him on various projects and goals in his life. In a way, these people seem like resources that need to be manipulated so he can achieve his objectives. Therefore, he believes that he must persuade them to do what he wants—the way he wants it. The self-actualized person knows that he cannot make choices for others—we all get to make our own choices. He may very well present his case or ideas to people with whom he is now in a relationship. However, if they choose not to participate with him, he knows his desires can still be fulfilled by being open to attracting someone new whose desires are more in harmony with his.

We may be in an intimate relationship, such as marriage, with someone who does not agree with us about the major concepts of life or about how this marriage relationship should work. The ordinary person sees that his only hope for resolution would be to exert pressure and attempt to *force* his partner to change her point of view.

The self-actualized person would see the situation from a different perspective. Having a clearer understanding of how life works, he would choose a different approach. First, he would become *very clear* about what he wanted. He might ask:

"Do I want to remain in this marriage regardless of how it affects me, or do I want to create an intimate relationship that is fulfilling?" The self-actualized person would probably choose fulfillment, and would begin by creating an ideal relationship for himself in his own mind. Knowing that we are all connected in the same *one mind,* this vision would create a *mind-form* that would start to attract the energy necessary to fulfill it. This is an expansive approach that knows no limits.

When we get clear about what we want and make a commitment to create it, a special energy emanates from us. This energy demands a *"like"* response. If our present partner can respond to this energy, he or she will probably do so. Whatever is necessary to bring this vision into our lives starts to unfold. The ordinary person would think that he must do something major, such as get a divorce or start looking for another partner to bring this vision about. The self-actualized person would know that this is neither necessary or appropriate. Whatever needs to happen will present itself. The self-actualized person would simply be open to any and all possibilities—trusting that whatever is best for all concerned will work out.

What we want in all of our relationships is to be involved with *like-minded* people. Not people exactly like us, but people who want the same kind of things we do and are willing to cooperate in bringing our mutual visions to fruition.

It is important to note here that there is a law which says *we get what we expect*. Or as the famous comedian Flip Wilson put it, *"What you see is what you get."* Believing in something does not make it true, but it does make it our experience. If we see our partner as disagreeable, possessive, demanding or incapable, this is the *version* of them that will be presented to us. We act as mirrors for each other. The people in our life will portray to us whatever we expect to see in them. Most of the time, this is not on any conscious or deliberate level. The other person may not have any awareness of what we see or believe about him or her—and what we believe may not even be true for him or her. Nevertheless, they will do whatever is necessary to help us to maintain our belief about them. Frequently, we project *limiting beliefs* onto those we are in relationship with. An example of this occurred in one of our classes where a couple was trying to improve their communications together. She complained that he didn't talk to her and wanted him to share more of his thoughts and feelings. Things didn't seem to be changing much until one day she discovered the problem. She said, "It just occurred to me that I still believe that John will not share things with me." She changed her belief, and soon their level of communicating and depth of sharing changed as well.

The ordinary person is totally unaware of the power of the mind and how it works with energy. The understanding of this *fourth dimension* which underlies all of the material world is accessed only through intuition.

Let's look at the issue of control from a different perspective. ***What happens if your child, even though he or she may be grown, is making choices that you totally disagree with? Do you feel a need to interfere?***

The ordinary person many times feels a need to control others, especially his children. It seldom works. The self-actualized person realizes that he is connected to his child on the level of mind. Therefore he works on the issues he has with them from this higher perspective. He knows that he cannot make choices for others. So he simply chooses to spend time and focus his attention on seeing the child as being well and happy rather than project an energy of frustration, impatience or judgement. The self-actualized parent does not attempt to control, in any way, the experiences that the child may need for his or her growth. In the outer realm, this parent is simply accepting and supportive. This does not mean that the parent does not express his thoughts, it simply means that he does not try to *interfere* by using any form of manipulation or control.

The ordinary person believes that he must convince, persuade, coerce, manipulate, or in some way control others. The self-actualized person knows that this is not at all necessary. He knows that he is in charge of his own life, and understands how energy works to bring people together for the benefit of all parties concerned. He knows that he attracts to himself whatever he believes in. Consequently he goes forward knowing that others in his experience will be cooperative in helping him to fulfill his desires.

Subject *The need to be RIGHT*

When someone disagrees with you, how important is it to prove to him/her that you are right? The ordinary person feels a need to be right. He believes that the information he has is correct and it is his *duty* to defend it. The ordinary person usually believes strongly in right and wrong. He also believes that there are very clear-cut lines between the two that everyone should be able to see.

The self-actualized person knows that right and wrong is a matter of perception. Even when we look at "the facts" they appear different to different people. We could have five people read the same book and give a report on it, and these reports would be as though they had read different books. The self-actualized person knows that if we expect others to see things as we do, we will be disappointed. Our perception is established by our own beliefs and past experiences. What could appear perfectly right to one person could seem totally wrong to another.

How much does it matter? Is it difficult for you to let others see things from there own points of view? The ordinary person identifies with his rightness. The ego gets involved, and feels more important and valuable if it considers itself to be right. It is highly invested in proving that its perception is the correct one. Since the self-actualized person knows that right and wrong are simply different perceptions, he does not have a strong need to convince anyone else that he is right.

I have seen people get into huge arguments about almost everything they encounter together. The need to be right seems to be greater than the need to be loved. Their self-worth is connected to their ability to know what is *right* in any particular situation. When we have only the senses and the intellect to guide us, we are unable to understand how beliefs and perceptions work. The self-actualized person understands that an absolute right or wrong does not exist, and that one person's perception is as good as another. He is guided to do what is right for him, knowing the same thing could be wrong for another. Therefore he has no need to convince anyone else that he is right. The ability to understand this has the potential to totally transform personal relationships.

Subject *Blame*

Do you have a tendency to blame someone else when things do not go the way you want? The ordinary person believes that others can and do control his life. They can claim to have done everything necessary to bring something about in their life, but someone else caused things to go wrong. He has a tendency to indulge in what we call the three deadly "C's": *condemn, complain, and criticize*. This behavior ***condemns*** other people's perceptions and actions, ***complains*** about how they affected him, and ***criticizes*** their choices.

The self-actualized person knows that he does not function as a separate entity. Understanding that ***everything in existence is energy,*** and that ***thought directs energy,*** the self-actualized person knows that if things do not turn out as he had planned, it is due to his lack of clarity or some other factor within himself. Consequently, he does not blame others or engage in the three deadly "C's".

Most of us have observed relationships where one party blames the other for whatever goes wrong for them. This produces unhealthy feelings of guilt or the need to prove one's innocence. Few relationships can withstand this kind of behavior.

The self-actualized person knows that we all create our *own* experiences through our *own* thoughts, beliefs and choices. Therefore, he takes full responsibility for his own experience, and clearly knows that if he has experiences that he does not like he can change them within himself.

Subject *The need for approval*

Do you feel a need to fully impress upon others your value or importance? The ordinary person, believing that others can make or break him, finds it necessary to impress people. He wants to be sure they know how important or valuable he is. He also needs a great deal of attention and praise.

The self-actualized person feels whole and complete within himself. He knows that others' thoughts affect him very little. He may receive a lot of attention and/or praise, which he will appreciate, but he has transcended needs. He realizes that how he feels about himself is most important. It is his own beliefs and intentions that determine his experiences and accomplishments.

The ordinary person is motivated by his needs. He will do whatever it takes to get the attention, appreciation and approval he craves. The self-actualized person is motivated only by his inner desire to accomplish or create something of value.

Subject *Attachment*

Are you attached to any of your relationships? By attachment I mean feeling that you need a particular person in your life in order to be complete. Again, the ordinary person sometimes thinks that he needs a primary relationship *in order to be OK,* and he depends on this relationship to make him a whole person.

The self-actualized person is whole and complete right within himself. He fully enjoys his relationships, but doesn't rely on anyone or anything to make him feel whole. He realizes that, indeed, there is nothing *really* outside himself since he is aware that we are all connected and expressions of the same source. This knowledge allows the self-actualized person to be totally free, and capable of allowing everyone else to make his or her own choices.

All of our relationships are for our growth, and we do indeed grow as a result of experiencing each of them. How well our relationships work depends on the consciousness of the people involved. Remember the ***law of attraction and repulsion.*** We attract to ourselves whatever we believe in.

We are always growing toward self-actualization and only from this level of functioning can we have truly harmonious and fulfilling relationships.

Nineteen

What's the Difference in Business?

To believe your own thought, to believe that what is true for you in your private heart is true for all men.

—Ralph Waldo Emerson

A business organization is a reflection of the people who make up the firm. We will now look at how most businesses are organized and operated from the perception of the ordinary person. We also want to explore how business organizations could change as more and more people become self-actualized.

Subject *Control*

Most organizations were created and designed to function around the concept of control. The organization must have a means of getting its employees to do whatever management decides is necessary to fulfill the organization's goals.

Control is often accomplished through manipulation or intimidation. It taps into the person's perceived needs and his fear of not being able to fulfill them.

The ordinary person believes that he needs a job in order to make a living. The business provides the job which pays the person a salary in exchange for performing a certain function that the company needs fulfilled.

Ordinary people control each other through fear. Most have a fear of losing something they believe they need. For the worker, it's the fear of losing his job. For the employer, it's the fear of losing a valuable employee. Other needs are also used for control purposes. An example would be the person who has a need for approval. In this case, a sufficient amount of attention and praise will get the job done.

When we are functioning only from the level of our senses and intellect, we believe that we must use some form of control to get others to cooperate with us.

The self-actualized person has transcended his needs. Therefore, he cannot be manipulated, intimidated or controlled in any way. Organizations need and want the talents and abilities of self-actualized people, but they also have a resistance to them because they do not fit into the organizational mold. Most managers do ***not*** understand how the self-actualized person functions or how to motivate him.

Subject *Motivation*

How do we motivate people? As we have seen, the ordinary person is driven by trying to meet his needs. The ordinary person has many needs *(see Maslow's Hierarchy of Needs, chapter 4).* He also believes that others can make or break him, or, in other words, that others have control over his life.

The self-actualized person has discovered that he fulfills his own needs from within himself. He may be interested in pursuing a particular job, and may do it exceptionally well, but he is motivated from within himself—usually his own inner desires to express himself or make a contribution. The self-actualized person can be enrolled in others' ideas, but only if they interest him, and he feels that they are in line with his purpose.

Subject *Integrity*

How important is integrity in business? We all know that integrity is valuable and that it affects trust and our ability to enroll others in our plans and goals. The ordinary person is still, however, burdened with finding a way to satisfy his needs. He believes that what others do, say, or think will affect his ability to fulfill his needs.

The self-actualized person always does right and never does wrong *(see Maslow's findings, chapter 4).* Right and wrong, of course, is a matter of perception, and the self-actualized person's perception of right or wrong may not be the same as that of the ordinary person. What we can say is that the self-actualized person is always true to himself.

Subject *Creativity/Innovation*

When we want to create something original, who is the best person for the job? What we call *genius* and *true originality* comes from the level of the superconscious. As we know, the superconscious communicates to us through intuition. The self-actualized person has developed his ability to access knowledge through intuition. Therefore, we find self-actualized people to be highly creative and innovative.

The ordinary person is limited to what he has been able to learn intellectually. He may be capable of manipulating elements to create new combinations and get different results, but he doesn't have access to true originality.

Subject *Change*

What happens when things are changing in an organization? The ordinary person doesn't like change. He likes to feel secure and change can upsets his sense of security. He becomes somewhat attached to the idea of how he has done things in the past, and has a very difficult time understanding that change can be good for him and his organization.

The self-actualized person does not become attached to external circumstances. He knows that ***everything in the relative world is always changing,*** and he is quite comfortable with change. He knows himself as both changing and non-changing. In order for change to occur there must be something stable that underlies the change. The self-actualized person knows the *stable* level therefore he knows that change is a part of the perfect order of life and is nothing to fear.

Subject *Stability*

Who can we count on? The ordinary person likes stability and also likes to maintain the status quo. When dramatic change occurs he often becomes over-stressed and therefore less capable of maintaining his balance and stability.

The self-actualized person is, by nature, balanced, and knows stability from within—being comfortable with both the *changing* and *unchanging* aspects of life. He knows that he is whole and complete, and nothing can change his ability to be in charge of his own life.

Subject *Flexibility*

Who can go with the flow? Since the self-actualized person knows that he is in charge of his own life, external changes do not dramatically affect him. Therefore, he can be very flexible and easily change directions when he sees the need for doing so.

The ordinary person lives by habit, and identifies more with the external world. Therefore, his ability to change course mid-stream is hampered. He does not understand that he is creating his own experiences, and this keeps him from gaining the flexibility that is necessary for change.

Subject *Longevity*

How long will a person stay with an organization? The ordinary person will stay as long as his needs are being fulfilled. The self-actualized person will stay as long as it holds his interest, and provides him a good opportunity to express himself.

Subject *Confidence*

What is the value of confidence and where do we find it? Confidence is a feeling of comfort within ourselves. The self-actualized person knows himself as an expression of the source, which is whole, complete and perfect. He sees his life unfolding from within himself, therefore, he seldom feels threatened by external circumstances.

The ordinary person may appear to be confident in the face of external confusion, but it is often an act. He does not know himself as whole and complete. He believes that others can, and do, control the experiences of his life.

Subject *Planning*

What role does planning play in our success? The ordinary person *knows* he needs to create and follow a plan to accomplish a specific task. He sets goals and builds a strategy he follows to meet these goals.

The self-actualized person also creates plans, but he looks at it from a different perspective. He first sets his goals, sees them already accomplished in his mind's eye, then he listens for intuitive guidance to direct him in designing his plan. He knows that getting clear about the goal is the most important step. When he does this, he puts the creative force of intelligence and energy into action. He follows through with the plan realizing that it can change. When he senses a need for a change he makes adjustments without feeling any attachment to the old plan.

Subject *Leadership*

How do the two differ in leadership roles? The ordinary leader has developed his ability to lead others, and in many cases does a very good job. However, he is still influenced by his own personal needs. He may also identify with his position and find it difficult to follow another's lead when it becomes necessary.

The self-actualized leader's abilities are innate, simply a part of who he is. Since he has transcended personal needs, he doesn't feel threatened by others' growth. In fact, he leads from a desire to *promote* growth in others. He is equally adept in following or leading. Since he does not identify with his position, he can easily follow another's lead if he agrees with the direction.

Subject *Entrepreneurial/Intrapreneurial Traits*

What are these traits and where do they come from? People who possess these traits are risk-takers. They are self-starters and willing to take full responsibility for whatever they create. Entrepreneurs are confident, creative, stable and flexible. Many ordinary people are entrepreneurs. It is just a greater challenge for them than it is for the self-actualized person.

The self-actualized person has taken charge of his own life, and is fully responsible for whatever he experiences. He possesses the traits necessary to become an entrepreneur. Whether he chooses to use these abilities in running a business or not is determined by his perception of his purpose in life.

Subject *Management Style*

What determines our management style? You may be familiar with style analysis tests which help us to become aware of how we cope with stressful situations. Our style of coping was developed when we were very young in response to how our parents rewarded our behavior. Did they praise us if we were being cute and entertaining, or were they looking for strict compliance and just "do what you were told?" In either case, we learned how to function by satisfying *their* needs. We usually carry this style of coping with us throughout our lives unless we become conscious of our style and make a determined effort to change it. If we can get conscious about it, we can often see that other people have their own needs and expectations, and we can choose to change our style to better position ourselves with others.

For the ordinary person, management style is usually something we have created for ourselves over time as we grow and determine what works best. It reflects our beliefs, which may or may not have changed over the period of our lifetime.

The self-actualized person will also have a management style, which has been created in much the same way. However, due to his ability to see things clearly and change easily, he can deal appropriately with people who have different styles. The self-actualized person has transcended needs, so his style will be a reflection of a sincere desire to lead, guide and help people to become the most they can be.

Subject *Independent/Interdependent*

We grow into both. The ordinary person wants to be independent—to be in charge of his own life—but is sometimes confused about how to explore both qualities at the same time.

The self-actualized person is independent in that he knows that he is whole and complete within himself, and is indeed in charge of the experiences in his life. He also knows that we are all connected, and that we are not separate entities—therefore, we are inherently interdependent.

Summary

Businesses, in general, are designed for and run by ordinary people since there are so many more of them in the world. We find a relative few self-actualized people in traditionally-run business organizations because these structures are not conducive to the free expressive life the self-actualized person chooses for himself. This encourages the self-actualized person to create and run his own business.

Yet, it is clear to see that the self-actualized person has many abilities that could greatly benefit business organizations. As more and more people become self-actualized they will create different kinds of businesses that are conducive to a free expression of life.

Life is simply easier, more enjoyable and more fulfilling for the fully developed person. Self-actualization is a natural outcome of focusing on our own personal growth. Organizations could greatly improve their effectiveness by helping people in the organization develop their full range of abilities.

The important leaders of the twenty-first century and beyond will be self-actualized people. It is a human potential that is available for everyone to enjoy.

20 Twenty

What's the Difference in Society?

All religions, arts and sciences are branches of the same tree. All these aspirations are directed toward ennobling man's life, uplifting it from the sphere of mere physical existence, leading the individual toward freedom.

—Albert Einstein

We have looked at the differences in how the ordinary person and the self-actualized person see the world and function in it. We know we are all moving toward self-actualization or maturity in our development. Many people are focusing their attention on their personal growth and are evolving very rapidly. Since everyone is connected, this growth affects all of us.

What kind of society will we create as more and more of us become self-actualized? How will it be different from what we see around us now?

There are people in our society today who are very immature. Their psychological abilities have not been developed to an awareness level of cause and effect—action and consequence. They are unable to see solutions to their many problems. Their cognitive abilities are not fully developed, therefore, their thoughts and actions come from fear and despair. It is very easy for these people to fall into destructive thoughts and behavior. Some of them are intellectually developed but not very psychologically advanced. They are not capable of fulfilling their needs, and many times make very bad choices in trying to do so.

Many people are focusing their attention on their personal growth and are evolving very rapidly. Since everyone is connected, this growth affects all of us.

On the other hand, we know that there are many ordinary people living their lives from a higher level than what we see on the evening news. These ordinary people, who make up the vast majority of our society, have reached a certain level of psychological maturity. They have discovered ways of fulfilling many of their needs. They are also aware of the needs of others, and to the best of their ability, they try to live their lives without infringing on others.

Self-actualized people are fully aware of their needs and the needs of others. They understand how these needs can be fulfilled from within each of us. Looking at life from a very different point-of-view, they live healthier, happier and more productive lives. Currently, self-actualized people are the smallest percentage of our population, but this number is growing.

We could draw a line with one end representing the totally immature and the other representing the fully mature person. Another way to look at this line would be to label one end ignorance and the other enlightenment. We will all find ourselves somewhere between the two ends. However, we are all evolving toward full maturity, which enables us to experience enlightenment.

Most of us have heard about the new age that is coming into the world. What does this mean? A major paradigm shift is taking place on all levels of society. We are experiencing and observing a change in the very pattern of what it means to be a human being. All kinds of possibilities are opening up to us.

In the book *The Way Ahead*, author Robert Thurman speaks of a prophecy made in the Far East many centuries ago, which predicts that some time around now the entire planet will usher in a Golden Age. During this time individuals all over the globe will find ideal conditions for pursuing personal evolution and advancement. Science and technology will develop unprecedented understanding and more effective methods of improving the quality of life. The earth will be restored and regain its abundance. All beings will become happy and healthy, growing intellectually and spiritually, living lives filled with meaning.

We are experiencing and observing a change in the very pattern of what it means to be a human being. All kinds of possibilities are opening up to us.

We believe that this time is rapidly approaching. There are two waves taking place in the world today simultaneously, an upward wave and a downward one. We see the downward wave expressed in all the crime, brutality, terrorism, and the incidents that are pushing us more and more into a police state. At the same time we see the upward wave bringing us to a totally different level of existence. The downward wave is made up of ignorant, unintelligent, destructive and death-oriented energy. The upward wave consists of all that is conscious, intelligent, creative and life-oriented in the world. Until recently the percentage of the population participating in the upward wave has been in the minority. That's OK. Fear and destruction spread numerically, which is slow. Light and life-supporting creativity spread exponentially, which is fast. Simple physics—the destructive wave will self-destruct and the creative wave will become exponential in its endless power to create. As more and more people focus their attention on self-development they will discover the fourth dimension—or spiritual dimension of life—and create a society that functions from a whole new level of understanding. Let's take a look at some of the things we might see in this new society.

Business: Today there exists a vast divide between our limited past and our boundless future. Business leaders are confused, with one foot on each side of the divide, because they lack a workable model for a knowledge-based economy.

A huge change is taking place in the business world as we see the shift from the *capital-centered economy* of the past to the *knowledge-centered economy* of the future. It's a new ball game with totally different rules. We need a new kind of player, one who is fully mature and capable of accessing creative ideas.

Fear and destruction spread numerically, which is slow. Life-affirming creativity spreads exponentially, which is fast. Simple physics—the destructive wave will diminish as the expansive wave dramatically builds into an endless power of positive possibility.

Here we need to distinguish between knowledge and information. We once believed that if we only had enough information, we could do anything. We can now access more information in a split second than we could ever use. It has finally become clear that information alone is not the answer. What we need is the ability to discern what information is valuable and how it fits into the big picture. Only the self-actualized person can truly see the big picture and how all the parts fit together. The intellect is limited in its ability to comprehend this big picture. Knowledge is the knowingness of how all the pieces fit together. We are now beginning to grasp the fact that knowledge, derived through intuition, is the source of all creativity and innovation. Former Shell executive Arie DeGeus says, *"The critical resource now is people and the knowledge they possess."*

As more and more of us become self-actualized we will be able to create businesses that function from a totally new perspective. All organizations start from a vision. Self-actualized people come from a desire to make a contribution to the world. They are more capable of envisioning organizations that serve all concerned, since they are able to see how we are all connected and affected by each other.

It is likely that we will see cooperation replace competition as a means to interact in this new world. The self-actualized person, knowing that we are all connected, is much more willing to share knowledge and work with others to fulfill the vision. They are also willing to share the recognition and praise.

Knowledge is the knowingness of how all parts fit together. We are beginning to grasp the fact that knowledge, derived through intuition, is the source of all creativity and innovation.

Understanding the principles of life, they are also willing to let the person or organization best qualified perform a particular task. The self-actualized person will just move on to a project where their talents are more useful. When fear is not a factor, organizations will function on a totally different level.

Government: Self-actualized people realize that there are laws of nature that govern our lives. As more and more people understand this concept, we will have less and less need for external governmental control. There are unavoidable consequences for making choices that are not in harmony with the laws of nature. The self-actualized person is aware of these laws and makes choices accordingly.

Real power comes from within, and we will begin to realize that external forces cannot regulate people's behavior. People change their behavior only when they have an understanding of why it needs to change. Crime will begin to diminish as more and more people become aware of the principles of life and how they work.

Government is based on a belief in external control. As people become aware of the power we each have within ourselves, governments as we have known in the past will no longer be appropriate.

Real power comes from within—external forces cannot regulate behavior. People change their behavior only when they have an understanding of why it needs to change.

War: The self-actualized person has no need for war. Since everything is energy, and we direct and form this energy through our thoughts, beliefs and expectations, we can create whatever we want. Resources are unlimited. We create our own boundaries—they are not created by others. The self-actualized person knows that the source of all of creation is Love, and we are all expressions of this Love, Intelligence and Energy. There is also a clear realization that Love is all powerful.

Traffic accidents: Would a self-actualized person drive irresponsibly? Would he drive with his senses impaired? It looks as if we can also look forward to fewer traffic accidents.

When we are not aware of our own wholeness, we attract people who mirror our misunderstandings back to us. This is perfect for our growth, but rarely produces relationships that are fun and rewarding.

Relationships: The closer to full maturity we become the better our relationships will be. When we are not aware of our own wholeness, we attract people who mirror our misunderstandings back to us. This is perfect for our growth, but rarely produces relationships that are fun and rewarding. When we feel whole and complete within ourselves we don't need others to do or say specific things to make us feel good about ourselves. When we are no longer needy it is easy to allow others to be who they are, and appreciate our differences as well as our similarities. As more and more of us become self-actualized, relationships will become more harmonious and fulfilling.

Families: Self-actualized people know themselves as expressions of Love. Love is the foundation for a family. They are aware that each individual gets to make his own choices, and according to the laws of nature, will experience the consequence of these choices. The self-actualized parent doesn't operate out of fear—therefore, fear is not passed on to the children.

Self-actualized individuals are simply ordinary people who have grown into full maturity. They have the ability to access knowledge from a source not available to others and are healthier, happier and more capable of creating the lives they want for themselves.

Summary

Self-actualized people are simply ordinary people who have grown in maturity. They are healthier, happier and more capable of creating the lives they want for themselves. They have the ability to access knowledge from a source not available to others. They see the world from a different perspective. At this point in time we can just begin to comprehend some of the changes that will take place in our society as more and more of us move into this realm of functioning. The world we have known in the past will change dramatically on all fronts.

I hope that this glimpse into future change has convinced you of the benefits of becoming self-actualized. Moving to this new level of functioning requires time and commitment, but I hope you can see that it is well worth the effort.

In *Part Three,* a process is provided for you to follow to reach this level of maturity. Many people have followed this process with remarkable results. As we all realize our oneness, we can create the lives we want for ourselves, and together we can create a whole new world for all of us.

21 TwentyOne

High Tech/High Touch

Go back into yourself.
Truth dwells in the inner man.

—St. Augustine

Technology has moved us into a whole new world. We can know and do things that we never dreamed possible in the past. It also demands that we evolve with it. Major discoveries often make our current abilities obsolete and so it is with the world of technology. Once we discovered how to make matches, the skill to start fires by rubbing sticks together was no longer needed. After the invention of hand-held calculators, it was no longer necessary to memorize our multiplication tables. With the advent of the internet, we can access libraries of information without even leaving our homes.

Things are moving faster and faster, and we are required to make immediate decisions on more and more issues. Since there isn't any time for analysis anymore—how do we make informed decisions?

Things are moving faster and faster, and we are required to make immediate decisions on more and more issues. There is no time for analysis anymore. *Then how do we make informed decisions? What new abilities do we need to develop?*

Life gets harder and harder every day for the ordinary person. This causes stress, and the stress continues to mount. The nervous system becomes overwhelmed, affecting our perception, causing us to make mistakes. Mistakes bring more stress, and life can seem to move into a downward cycle. If we are doctors, nurses, pharmacists or pilots, our mistakes can cost lives. For most of us our mistakes are less critical, but they still affect the quality of our lives.

What can be done about it? When we choose a lifestyle that focuses our attention on releasing the stress that builds up in the nervous system on a daily basis the system becomes stronger. This strong nervous system provides clarity in perception, which helps us to achieve our goals. Achieving our goals makes us even stronger, and we begin to create an upward spiral in our ability to make better lives for ourselves.

We must develop our intuition in order to function well in a high-tech world. We can now get more information in a split second than we can ever use. It is more important than ever to determine the value of the information we get, and know what information will be helpful to us. The intellect alone is not very effective in this high tech world. However, we can choose to develop our intuitive abilities which allows us to make immediate decisions which are always in our best interest. Intuitively we can *know*. The intellect can only think or use reason and logic which is much too slow for the new world in which we find ourselves.

What is important?

Recently, I read an article about several people who were now billionaires many times over. They were young and had made an enormous amount of money as a result of technology.

However, the article said they were all severely depressed and could find no meaning to life.

If you could be granted one request for your life, what would you ask for? Most of us would probably ask for happiness. When it comes down to it, the pursuit of happiness is one of the strongest drives we have as human beings. *Have we been looking in the wrong places for our happiness?*

The pursuit of happiness is one of the strongest drives we have as human beings, but have we been looking in ALL the wrong places to find it?

The technology we now enjoy is a major evolutionary step for us as a society. Technology seems to exist outside ourselves. It represents an outward direction—pointing to a world beyond ourselves—a place where we seem to focus most of our attention. We have gained *outer* success, but what about what is most important *within* us.

Technology and everything in the outer world is only a means for us to use in our own growth. It is the inner development that makes life really worthwhile. The self-actualized person functions well in the outer world, because he knows *both* the inner and the outer worlds. Understanding how they relate to each other, he recognizes what is important. He has conquered fear, which allows him to feel peaceful, whole and complete regardless of what appears to be happening in the outer world. He knows that either world can be changed from within himself.

The soft stuff—*high touch*—is actually where all the power lies. We usually think of high touch as our relationship to other people—the ones that help us to keep from getting lost among all of the machines and *mechanical routines* in our lives. High touch most importantly refers to our relationship with ourselves.

Now, please return to page one and re-read this book. Every time you read it you will discover more about who you are, how you function and how to create the life you want for yourself.

We have all the power we need right within ourselves to create our lives to be just the way we want them to be. *What kind of life will you create?* It is all a matter of choice. I hope this book has given you new insights and techniques you can use for creating the life you want.

The Unlimited Futures mission is to *"provide programs and an environment which allows each of us to discover who we are, how we function, our purpose and how to accomplish it. This will build a network of people around the world who are creating the lives they want for themselves and are actively helping others do the same."*

Thank you for helping me fulfill *my* purpose.

Now, please return to page one and re-read this book. Every time you read it you will discover more about who you are, how you function and how to create the life you want for yourself.

NOTE: Make a copy of the personal contract on page 231. Read it, fill it out and sign it. It would be wise to rework and renew your *Contract with mySelf* on a regular basis. As you change, grow and develop new awareness, you will be willing to commit to yourself on deeper and deeper levels.

Enjoy your daily routine and the wonderful life you are creating.

Contract with mySelf

Date __________

Check only the statements you are willing to fully COMMIT yourself to

I, ____

___ **am committed to practicing the *Unlimited Futures* Program (the energizers, breathing exercises, meditation and work with my choices) TWICE a day—everyday.** I choose to change my lifestyle so that I can more elegantly create my life *exactly* the way I want it to be. I realize that doing the routine twice a day will give me the strength to make these changes possible. I am dedicated to refining my nervous system and the mind/body energy so I can fulfill my needs and become a fully-engaged, self-actualized person.

___ **am committed to working the *Unlimited Futures* Program ONCE a day—everyday.** I choose to begin strengthening my mind/body energy and release the stress stored in my nervous system. I realize that this new routine will help minimize the effects of stress in my life and help me open up to new ways of creating what I want.

___ **am committed to working with the materials I have discovered in the *Unlimited Futures* book.** I am willing to practice the Program when I feel guided to do so, understanding that it will begin to open me up to more and more awareness about how I create my life and become more clear about my personal choices.

___ choose to focus more on loving myself, allowing this energy to transform my life.
___ choose to choose—I am committed to exploring the power of personal choice.
___ choose to reach for perfect physical, emotional, mental and spiritual health.
___ choose to discover new ways to be free in the ways I live my life.
___ choose to be true to myself—to be honest about my thoughts, feelings, needs and choices.
___ choose to be the *Observer*—being *consciously* aware of the ways I interact with the world around me—and observant of how it responds to where I place my focus.
___ choose to be a *Master Receiver*—being willing and open to receive the life I desire.

Signed

____

Index

Pages numbers ***in bold italics*** indicate pages with illustrations

About the Author

Bobbie R. Stevens, Ph.D., is cofounder and president of *Unlimited Futures, LLC,* an organization that has been providing programs for the development of human potential for more than twenty years. She holds doctorates in both psychology and business management. After a successful career in business, she moved into the field of industrial psychology, and in 1979 she founded the *American Institute for Creativity, Health and Productivity.* Dr. Stevens' work has resulted in a higher quality of life for thousands of individuals, and her *Executive Development Programs* have made outstanding contributions to many Fortune 500 companies as well as to numerous smaller ones. Dr. Stevens lives and works with her husband, Dr. Dean Portinga, in Naples, Florida.

More Information

For more information on the *Unlimited Futures* programs, to give us feedback or to subscribe to our newsletter, please visit our website at: *www.theufb.com.*